Martin Schoeberl

JOP: A Java Optimized Processor for
Embedded Real-Time Systems

Martin Schoeberl

JOP: A Java Optimized Processor for Embedded Real-Time Systems

VDM Verlag Dr. Müller

Imprint

Bibliographic information by the German National Library: The German National Library lists this publication at the German National Bibliography; detailed bibliographic information is available on the Internet at
http://dnb.d-nb.de.

Cover image: www.purestockx.com

Published 2008 Saarbrücken

Publisher:
VDM Verlag Dr. Müller Aktiengesellschaft & Co. KG, Dudweiler Landstr. 125 a,
66123 Saarbrücken, Germany,
Phone +49 681 9100-698, Fax +49 681 9100-988,
Email: info@vdm-verlag.de
Zugl.: Vienna University of Technology, PhD Thesis, 2005

Produced in Germany by:
Reha GmbH, Dudweilerstrasse 72, D-66111 Saarbrücken
Schaltungsdienst Lange o.H.G., Zehrensdorfer Str. 11, 12277 Berlin, Germany
Books on Demand GmbH, Gutenbergring 53, 22848 Norderstedt, Germany

Impressum

Bibliografische Information der Deutschen Nationalbibliothek: Die Deutsche Nationalbibliothek verzeichnet diese Publikation in der Deutschen Nationalbibliografie; detaillierte bibliografische Daten sind im Internet über http://dnb.d-nb.de abrufbar.

Coverbild: www.purestockx.com

Erscheinungsjahr: 2008
Erscheinungsort: Saarbrücken

Verlag: VDM Verlag Dr. Müller Aktiengesellschaft & Co. KG, Dudweiler Landstr. 125 a,
D- 66123 Saarbrücken,
Telefon +49 681 9100-698, Telefax +49 681 9100-988,
Email: info@vdm-verlag.de
Zugl.: Vienna University of Technology, PhD Thesis, 2005

Herstellung in Deutschland:
Schaltungsdienst Lange o.H.G., Zehrensdorfer Str. 11, D-12277 Berlin
Books on Demand GmbH, Gutenbergring 53, D-22848 Norderstedt
Reha GmbH, Dudweilerstrasse 72, D-66111 Saarbrücken

ISBN: 978-3-8364-8086-4

Abstract

Compared to software development for desktop systems, current software design practice for embedded systems is still archaic. C/C++ and even assembler are used on top of a small real-time operating system. Many of the benefits of Java, such as safe object references, the notion of concurrency as a first-class language construct, and its portability, have the potential to make embedded systems much safer and simpler to program. However, Java technology is seldom used in embedded systems, due to the lack of acceptable real-time performance.

This thesis presents a Java processor designed for time-predictable execution of real-time tasks. JOP (Java Optimized Processor) is the implementation of the Java virtual machine in hardware. JOP is intended for applications in embedded real-time systems and the primary implementation technology is in a field programmable gate array. This research demonstrates that a hardware implementation of the Java virtual machine results in a small design for resource-constrained devices.

Architectural advancements in modern processor designs increase average performance with features such as pipelines, caches and branch prediction. However, these features complicate worst-case execution time (WCET) analysis and lead to very conservative WCET estimates. This thesis tackles this problem from the architectural perspective – by introducing a processor architecture in which simpler and more accurate WCET analysis is more important than average case performance.

This thesis evaluates the issues surrounding the use of standard Java for real-time applications. In order to overcome some of the issues with standard Java, a profile for real-time Java is defined. Tight integration of the real-time scheduler with the supporting processor result in an efficient platform for Java in embedded real-time systems.

The proposed processor and the Java real-time profile have been used with success to implement several commercial real-time applications.

Contents

1 Introduction

This thesis introduces the concept of a Java processor for embedded real-time systems, in particular the design of a small processor for resource-constrained devices with time-predictable execution of Java programs. This Java processor is called JOP – which stands for Java Optimized Processor –, based on the assumption that a full native implementation of all Java bytecode instructions is not a useful approach.

1.1 Justification for Development

To justify Java's use in embedded real-time systems we quote from a document published by the National Institute of Standards and Technology [47]:

- Java's higher level of abstraction allows for increased programmer productivity (although recognizing that the tradeoff is runtime efficiency)

- Java is relatively easier to master than C++

- Java is relatively secure, keeping software components (including the JVM itself) protected from one another

- Java supports dynamic loading of new classes

- Java is highly dynamic, supporting object and thread creation at runtime

- Java is designed to support component integration and reuse

- The Java technologies have been developed with careful consideration, erring on the conservative side using concepts and techniques that have been scrutinized by the community

- The Java programming language and Java platforms support application portability

- The Java technologies support distributed applications

- Java provides well-defined execution semantics

Based on the NIST document, the Real-Time for Java Experts Group has published the Real Time Specification for Java (RTSJ) [8] to add real-time extensions to Java.

Despite the above, to date Java is rarely used in embedded real-time systems. High resource requirements for the Java virtual machine and unpredictable real-time behavior are the main issues surrounding the use of Java for embedded systems. This thesis addresses both issues, and the proposed Java processor makes a strong case for the use of Java in embedded systems.

1.2 Embedded Real-Time Systems

An embedded system is a special-purpose computer system that is part of a larger system or machine. An embedded system is designed to perform a narrow range of functions with no, or minimal user intervention.

Since many embedded systems are produced in large quantities, the need to reduce costs is a major concern. Embedded systems often have significant energy constraints, and many are battery-powered. As a result of these constraints, embedded systems use a slow processor and small memory size to minimize costs and energy consumption.

Embedded systems interact with the environment and often have to produce output within a given timeframe. Therefore, most embedded systems are real-time systems. Here is a general definition of a real-time system (John A. Stankovic [88]):

> In real-time computing the correctness of the system depends not only on the logical result of the computation but also on the time at which the result is produced.

However, it should be noted that 'real-time' does not mean 'really fast'. In pure real-time systems (i.e. without non real-time tasks), there is no additional value in producing results earlier than required.

Embedded real-time systems often have to handle concurrent tasks, such as communication, calculating values for a control loop, user interface and supervision. A natural way to handle these concurrent jobs is to model them as individual tasks. These tasks are executed on a preemptive multi-tasking system. Each task is assigned a priority and the multi-tasking system is responsible for scheduling individual tasks according to their priority.

To fulfil the time constraints for a real-time system, an appropriate schedule needs to be found. This problem was solved in the classic paper by Liu and Layland [61] on independent periodic tasks. The optimal priority assignment for a set of tasks is called the rate monotonic priority order, in which a task with a shorter period is assigned a higher priority. If the Worst-Case Execution Time (WCET) of each task is known, the schedule is feasible and all tasks will meet their deadline[1], if:

$$\frac{C_1}{T_1} + \cdots + \frac{C_n}{T_n} \leq U(n) = n(2^{\frac{1}{n}} - 1)$$

where

$$C_i = \text{worst-case execution time of } task_i$$
$$T_i = \text{period of } task_i$$
$$U(n) = \text{utilization bound for } n \text{ tasks.}$$

In theory, this test is both elegant and simple. For concrete systems, two issues have to be solved:

- There are very few systems in existence that do not require communication between tasks. As a result, tasks cannot be seen as independent and blocking needs to be incorporated into the schedulability analysis.

- The WCET of each task has to be known. This is not a trivial task. Simple measurements of execution times never fully guarantee a correct value. The tasks therefore have to be analyzed using the correct model of the target system. It is almost impossible to provide an accurate and correct model of modern processors and memory systems.

Several standard textbooks on real-time systems [51, 10] deal with the first issue. JOP is intended to resolve the second issue. It should be noted that there are a number of scheduling approaches and schedulability tests. However, as a rule, these approaches all assume that the WCET of each task is known.

1.3 Research Objectives and Contributions

This thesis presents a hardware implementation of the Java Virtual Machine (JVM), targeting small embedded systems with real-time constraints. The processor is designed from the ground up for low WCET of bytecodes, in order to give tasks low WCET values. The following list summarizes the research objectives for the proposed Java processor:

---

[1] The period of a periodic task is the time between consecutive activations of the task. The deadline of the task is assumed to be at the end of the tasks period.

Primary Objectives:

- Time-predictable Java platform for embedded real-time systems

- Small design that fits into a low-cost FPGA

- A working processor, not merely a proposed architecture

Secondary Objectives:

- Acceptable performance compared with mainstream non real-time Java systems

- A flexible architecture that allows different configurations for different application domains

- Definition of a real-time profile for Java

Contributions:

JOP is a stack computer with its own instruction set, called microcode in this thesis. Java bytecodes are translated into microcode instructions or sequences of microcode. The difference between the JVM and JOP is best described as the following:

> The JVM is a CISC stack architecture, whereas JOP is a RISC stack architecture.

JOP will help to increase the acceptance of Java for embedded real-time systems. JOP is implemented as a soft-core in a Field Programmable Gate Array (FPGA). Using an FPGA as the processor for embedded systems is uncommon, because of the high costs, compared with a microcontroller. However, if the core is small enough, unused FPGA resources can be used to implement periphery in the FPGA, resulting in a lower chip count and hence lower overall costs.

The thesis' main contributions are as follows:

- The execution time for Java bytecodes can be exactly predicted in terms of the number of clock cycles. There is no mutual dependency between consecutive bytecodes. Therefore, no pipeline analysis – with possible unbound timing effects – is necessary. These properties greatly simplify low-level WCET analysis.

  In order to fill the gap between processor speed and the memory access time, caches are mandatory. In Section 5.8, a novel way to organize an instruction cache, as *method cache*, is provided. This method cache is simple to analyze with respect to worst-case behavior and still provides a substantial performance gain when compared against a solution without an instruction cache.

The proposed processor architecture results in a predictable and high-performance execution of real-time tasks in Java, without the resource implications and unpredictability of a JIT-compiler.

- JOP is microprogrammed using a novel way of mapping bytecodes to microcode addresses. This mapping has zero overheads, even for complex bytecodes.

A two-level stack cache, described in Section 5.5, which fits to the embedded memory technologies of current FPGAs and ASICs, ensures the fast execution of basic instructions with minimum resource requirements. Fill and spill of the stack cache is subjected to microcode control and therefore time-predictable.

JOP is the smallest hardware implementation of the JVM available to date. This fact enables low-cost FPGAs to be used in embedded systems. The resource usage of JOP can be configured to trade size against performance for different application domains.

- The definition of standard Java does not fit hard real-time applications. Therefore, a real-time profile for Java (with restrictions) is defined in Section 6.1 and implemented on JOP. Tight integration of the scheduler and the hardware that generates schedule events results in low latency and low jitter of the task dispatch.

In this profile, hardware interrupts are represented as asynchronous events with associated threads. These events are subject to the control of the scheduler and can be incorporated into the priority assignment and schedulability analysis in the same way as normal application tasks.

- One contribution made as part of this thesis is the concrete implementation of the proposed architecture. The author is aware that it is not usually considered necessary to provide a complete implementation as part of a thesis. However, it is the opinion of the author that a simulation-only approach would lead to mistakes or small glitches. By providing a concrete implementation, we are not only confronted with the full complexity of real-life processes, but also with one or more major issues that would often be generously overlooked in a simulation. In Section 7.5, the usage of JOP in a real-world application is described.

1.4 Outline of the Thesis

Chapter 2 provides background information on the Java programming language and the execution environment, the Java virtual machine, for Java applications.

The related work is presented in Chapter 3. Different hardware solutions from both academia and industry for accelerating Java in embedded systems are analyzed. This chapter concludes with the research question.

Standard Java is not suitable for the resource-constrained world of embedded systems. Chapter 4 gives an overview of the different restrictions of Java for embedded and real-time systems.

Chapter 5 is the main chapter of this thesis in which the architecture of JOP is described. The motivation behind different design decisions is given.

A Java processor alone is not a complete JVM. Chapter 6 describes the runtime environment on top of JOP, including the definition of a real-time profile for Java and a framework for a user-defined scheduler in Java.

In Chapter 7, JOP is evaluated with respect to size, performance and WCET. This is followed by a description of the first commercial real-world application of JOP.

Finally, in Chapter 8, the work undertaken is reviewed and the major contributions of this thesis are presented. This chapter concludes with directions for future research using JOP and real-time Java.

2 Java and the Java Virtual Machine

Java technology consists of the Java language definition, a definition of the standard library, and the definition of an intermediate instruction set with an accompanying execution environment. This combination helps to make *write once, run anywhere* possible.

The following chapter gives a short overview of the Java programming language. A more detailed description of the Java Virtual Machine (JVM) and the explanation of the JVM instruction set, the so-called bytecodes follows. The exploration of dynamic instruction counts of typical Java programs can be found in Section 5.1.

2.1 Java

Java is a relatively new and popular programming language. The main features that have helped Java achieve success are listed below:

Simple and object oriented: Java is a simple programming language that appears very similar to C. This 'look and feel' of C means that programmers that know C, can switch to Java without difficulty. Java provides a simplified object model with single inheritance[1].

Portability: To accommodate the diversity of operating environments, the Java compiler generates bytecodes – an architecture neutral intermediate format. To guarantee platform independence, Java specifies the sizes of its basic data types and the behavior of its arithmetic operators. A Java interpreter, the Java virtual machine, is available on various platforms to help make 'write once, run anywhere' possible.

Availability: Java is not only available for different operating systems, it is available at no cost. The runtime system and the compiler can be downloaded from Sun's website for Windows, Linux and Solaris. Sophisticated development environments, such as Netbeans or Eclipse, are available under the GNU Public License.

---

[1] Java has *single inheritance* of *implementation* – only one class can be extended. However, a class can implement several interfaces, which means that Java has *multiple interface inheritance*.

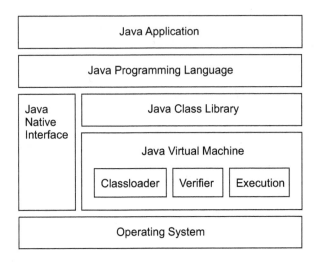

Figure 2.1: Java system overview

Library: The complete Java system includes a rich class library to increase programming productivity. Besides the functionality from a C standard library, it also contains other tools, such as collection classes and a GUI toolkit.

Built-in multithreading: Java supports multithreading at the language level: the library provides the Thread class, the language provides the keyword synchronized for critical sections and the runtime system provides monitor and condition lock primitives. The system libraries have been written to be thread-safe: the functionality provided by the libraries is available without conflicts due to multiple concurrent threads of execution.

Safety: Java provides extensive compile-time checking, followed by a second level of runtime checking. The memory management model is simple – objects are created with the new operator. There are no explicit pointer data types and no pointer arithmetic, but there is automatic garbage collection. This simple memory management model eliminates a large number of the programming errors found in C and C++ programs. A restricted runtime environment, the so-called *sandbox*, is available when executing small Java applications in Web browsers.

As can be seen in Figure 2.1, Java consists of three main components:

1. The Java programming language as defined in [33]

2. The class library, defined as part of the Java specification. All implementations of Java have to contain the library defined by Sun

3. The Java virtual machine (defined in [60]) that loads, verifies and executes the binary representation (the *class file*) of a Java program

The Java native interface supports functions written in C or C++. This combination is sometimes called *Java technology* to emphasize the fact that Java is more than just another object-oriented language.

However, a number of issues have hindered a broad acceptance of Java. The original presentation of Java as an Internet language led to the misconception that Java was not a general-purpose programming language. Another obstacle was the first implementation of the JVM as an interpreter. Execution of Java programs was *very* slow compared to compiled C/C++ programs. Although advances in its runtime technology, in particular the just-in-time compiler, have closed the performance gap, it is still a commonly held view that Java is slow.

2.1.1 History

The Java programming language originated as part of a research project to develop software for network devices and embedded systems. In the early '90s, Java, which was originally known as Oak [65, 67], was created as a programming tool for a consumer device that we would today call a PDA. The device (known as *7) was a small SPARC-based hardware device with a tiny embedded OS. However, the *7 was not issued as a product and Java was officially released in 1995 as a new language for the Internet (to be integrated into Netscape's browser). Over the years, Java technology has become a programming tool for desktop applications, web servers and server applications. These application domains resulted in the split of the Java platform into the Java standard edition (J2SE) and the enterprise edition (J2EE) in 1999. With every new release, the library (defined as part of the language) continued to grow. Java for embedded systems was clearly not an area Sun was interested in pursuing. However, with the arrival of mobile phones, Sun again became interested in this embedded market. Sun defined different subsets of Java, which have now been combined into the Java Micro Edition (J2ME). A detailed description of the J2ME follows in Section 4.3.

2.1.2 The Java Programming Language

The Java programming language is a general-purpose object-oriented language. Java is related to C and C++, but with a number of aspects omitted. Java is a strongly

Type	Description
boolean	either true or false
char	16-bit Unicode character (unsigned)
byte	8-bit integer (signed)
short	16-bit integer (signed)
int	32-bit integer (signed)
long	64-bit integer (signed)
float	32-bit floating-point (IEEE 754-1985)
double	64-bit floating-point (IEEE 754-1985)

Table 2.1: Java primitive data types

typed language, which means that type errors can be detected at compile time. Other errors, such as wrong indices in an array, are checked at runtime. The problematic[2] *pointer* in C and explicit deallocation of memory is completely avoided. The pointer is replaced by a *reference*, i.e. an abstract pointer to an object. Storage for an object is allocated from the heap during creation of the object with new. Memory is freed by automatic storage management, typically using a garbage collector. The garbage collector avoids memory leaks from a missing free() and the safety problems exposed by dangling pointers.

The types in Java are divided into two categories: primitive types and reference types. Table 2.1 lists the available primitive types. Method local variables, class fields and object fields contain either a primitive type value or a reference to an object.

Classes and class instances, the objects, are the fundamental data and code organization structures in Java. There are no global variables or functions as there are in C/C++. Each method belongs to a class. This 'everything belongs to a class or an object' combined with the class naming convention, as suggested by Sun, avoids name conflicts in even the largest applications.

New classes can extend exactly one superclass. Classes that do not explicitly extend a superclass become direct subclasses of Object, the root of the whole class tree. This single inheritance model is extended by *interfaces*. Interfaces are abstract classes that only define method signatures and provide no implementation. A concrete class can implement several interfaces. This model provides a simplified form of multiple inheritance.

Java supports multitasking through *threads*. Each thread is a separate flow of control, executing concurrently with all other threads. A thread contains the method

---

[2]C pointers represent memory addresses as data. Pointer arithmetic and direct access to memory leads to common and hard-to-find program errors.

stack as thread local data – all objects are shared between threads. Access conflicts to shared data are avoided by the proper use of synchronized methods or code blocks.

Java programs are compiled to a machine-independent bytecode representation as defined in [60]. Although this intermediate representation is defined for Java, other programming languages (e.g. ADA [13]) can also be compiled into Java bytecodes.

2.2 The Java Virtual Machine

The Java virtual machine (JVM) is a definition of an abstract computing machine that executes bytecode programs. The JVM specification [60] defines three elements:

- An instruction set and the meaning of those instructions – the *bytecodes*

- A binary format – the *class file* format. A class file contains the bytecodes, a symbol table and other ancillary information

- An algorithm to *verify* that a class file contains valid programs

In the solution presented in this thesis, the class files are verified, linked and transformed into an internal representation before being executed on JOP. This transformation is performed with JavaCodeCompact and is not executed on JOP. We will therefore omit the description of the class file and the verification process.

The instruction set of the JVM is stack-based. All operations take their arguments from the stack and put the result onto the stack. Values are transferred between the stack and various memory areas. We will discuss these memory areas first, followed by an explanation of the instruction set.

2.2.1 Memory Areas

The JVM contains various runtime data areas. Some of these areas are shared between threads, whereas other data areas exist separately for each thread.

Method area: The method area is shared among all threads. It contains static class information such as field and method data, the code for the methods and the constant pool. The constant pool is a per-class table, containing various kinds of constants such as numeric values or method and field references. The constant pool is similar to a symbol table.

Part of this area, the code for the methods, is very frequently accessed (during instruction fetch) and therefore is a good candidate for caching.

Heap: The heap is the data area where all objects and arrays are allocated. The heap is shared among all threads. A garbage collector reclaims storage for objects.

JVM stack: Each thread has a private stack area that is created at the same time as the thread. The JVM stack is a logical stack that contains following elements:

1. A frame that contains return information for a method

2. A local variable area to hold local values inside a method

3. The operand stack, where all operations are performed

Although it is not strictly necessary to allocate all three elements to the same type of memory we will see in Section 5.5 that the argument-passing mechanism regulates the layout of the JVM stack.

Local variables and the operand stack are accessed as frequently as registers in a standard processor. A Java processor shall provide some caching mechanism of this data area.

The memory areas are similar to the various segments in conventional processes (e.g. the method code is analogous to the 'text' segment). However, the operand stack replaces the registers in a conventional processor.

2.2.2 JVM Instruction Set

The instruction set of the JVM contains 201 different instructions [60], the *bytecodes* that can be grouped into the following categories:

Load and store: Load instructions push values from the local variables onto the operand stack. Store instructions transfer values from the stack back to local variables. 70 different instructions belong to this category. Short versions (single byte) exist to access the first four local variables. There are unique instructions for each basic type (`int`, `long`, `float`, `double` and `reference`). This differentiation is necessary for the bytecode verifier, but is not needed during execution. For example `iload`, `fload` and `aload` all transfer one 32-bit word from a local variable to the operand stack.

Arithmetic: The arithmetic instructions operate on the values found on the stack and push the result back onto the operand stack. There are arithmetic instructions for `int`, `float` and `double`. There is no direct support for `byte`, `short` or `char` types. These values are handled by `int` operations and have to be converted back before being stored in a local variable or an object field.

Type conversion: The type conversion instructions perform numerical conversions between all Java types: as implicit widening conversions (e.g. int to long, float or double) or explicit (by casting to a type) narrowing conversions.

Object creation and manipulation: Class instances and arrays (that are also objects) are created and manipulated with different instructions. Objects and class fields are accessed with type-less instructions.

Operand stack manipulation: All direct stack manipulation instructions are type-less and operate on 32-bit or 64-bit entities on the stack. Examples of these instructions are dup, to duplicate the top operand stack value, and pop, to remove the top operand stack value.

Control transfer: Conditional and unconditional branches cause the JVM to continue execution with an instruction other than the one immediately following. Branch target addresses are specified relative to the current address with a signed 16-bit offset. The JVM provides a complete set of branch conditions for int values and references. Floating-point values and type long are supported through compare instructions. These compare instructions result in an int value on the operand stack.

Method invocation and return: The different types of methods are supported by four instructions: invoke a class method, invoke an instance method, invoke a method that implements an interface and an invokespecial for an instance method that requires special handling, such as private methods or a superclass method.

A bytecode consists of one instruction byte followed by optional operand bytes. The length of the operand is one or two bytes, with the following exceptions: multianewarray contains 3 operand bytes; invokeinterface contains 4 operand bytes, where one is redundant and one is always zero; lookupswitch and tableswitch (used to implement the Java switch statement) are variable-length instructions; and goto_w and jsr_w are followed by a 4 byte branch offset, but neither is used in practice as other factors limit the method size to 65535 bytes.

2.2.3 Methods

A Java *method* is equivalent to a *function* or *procedure* in other languages. In object oriented terminology this *method* is *invoked* instead of *called*. We will use *method* and *invoke* in the remainder of this text. In Java and the JVM, there are five types of methods:

- Static or class methods

- Virtual methods

- Interface methods

- Class initialization

- Constructor of the parent class (`super()`)

For these five types there are only four different bytecodes:

invokestatic: A class method (declared static) is invoked. As the target does not depend on an object, the method reference can be resolved at load/link time.

invokevirtual: An object reference is resolved and the corresponding method is invoked. The resolution is usually done with a dispatch table per class containing all implemented and inherited methods. With this dispatch table, the resolution can be performed in constant time.

invokeinterface: An interface allows Java to emulate multiple inheritance. A class can implement several interfaces, and different classes (that have no inheritance relation) can implement the same interface. This flexibility results in a more complex resolution process. One method of resolution is a search through the class hierarchy that results in a variable, and possibly lengthy, execution time. A constant time resolution is possible by assigning every interface method a unique number. Each class that implements an interface needs its own table with unique positions for each interface method of the *whole* application.

invokespecial: Invokes an instance method with special handling for superclass, private, and instance initialization. This bytecode catches many different cases. This results in expensive checks for common private instance methods.

2.2.4 Implementation of the JVM

There are several different ways to implement a virtual machine. The following list presents these possibilities and analyses how appropriate they are for embedded devices.

```
for (;;) {
    instr = bcode[pc++];
    switch (instr) {
        ...
        case IADD:
            tos = stack[sp]+stack[sp−1];
            —sp;
            stack[sp] = tos;
            break;
        ...
    }
}
```

Listing 2.1: Typical JVM interpreter loop

Interpreter: The simplest realization of the JVM is a program that interprets the bytecode instructions. The interpreter itself is usually written in C and is therefore easy to port to a new computer system. The interpreter is very compact, making this solution a primary choice for resource-constrained systems. The main disadvantage is the high execution overhead. From a code fragment of the typical interpreter loop, as shown in Listing 2.1, we can examine the overhead: The emulation of the stack in a high-level language results in three memory accesses for a simple iadd bytecode. The instruction is decoded through an indirect jump. Indirect jumps are still a burden for standard branch prediction logic.

Just-In-Time Compilation: Interpreting JVMs can be enhanced with just-in-time (JIT) compilers. A JIT compiler translates Java bytecodes to native instructions during runtime. The time spent on compilation is part of the application execution time. JIT compilers are therefore restricted in their optimization capacity. To reduce the compilation overhead, current JVMs operate in mixed mode: Java methods are executed in interpreter mode and the call frequency is monitored. Often-called methods, the hot spots, are then compiled to native code.

JIT compilation has several disadvantages for embedded systems, notably that a compiler (with the intrinsic memory overhead) is necessary on the target system. Due to compilation during runtime, execution times are not predictable[3].

Batch Compilation: Java can be compiled, in advance, to the native instruction set of the target. Precompiled libraries are linked with the application during runtime. This is quite similar to C/C++ applications with shared libraries. This solution undermines the flexibility of Java: dynamic class loading during runtime. However, this is not a major concern for embedded systems.

Hardware Implementation: A Java processor is the implementation of the JVM in hardware. The JVM bytecode is the native instruction set of such a processor. This solution can result in quite a small processor, as a stack architecture can be implemented very efficiently. A Java processor is memory-efficient as an interpreting JVM, but avoids the execution overhead. The main disadvantage of a Java processor is the lack of capability to execute C/C++ programs.

2.3 Summary

Java is a unique combination of the language definition, a rich class library and a runtime environment. A Java program is compiled to bytecodes that are executed by a Java virtual machine. Strong typing, runtime checks and avoidance of pointers make Java a *safe* language. The intermediate bytecode representation simplifies porting of Java to different computer systems. An interpreting JVM is easy to implement and needs few system resources. However, the execution speed suffers from interpreting. JVMs with a just-in-time compiler are state-of-the-art for desktop and server systems. These compilers require large amounts of memory and have to be ported for each processor architecture, which means they are not the best choice for embedded systems. A Java processor is the implementation of the JVM as a concrete machine. A Java processor avoids the slow execution model of an interpreting JVM and the memory requirements of a compiler, thus making it an interesting execution system for Java in embedded systems.

---

[3]Even if the time for the compilation is known, the WCET for a method has to include the compile time!

3 Related Work

Two different approaches can be found to improve Java bytecode execution by hardware. The first type operates as a Java coprocessor in conjunction with a general-purpose microprocessor. This coprocessor is placed in the instruction fetch path of the main processor and translates Java bytecodes to sequences of instructions for the host CPU or directly executes basic Java bytecodes. The complex instructions are emulated by the main processor. Java chips in the second category replace the general-purpose CPU. All applications therefore have to be written in Java. While the first type enables systems with mixed code capabilities, the additional component significantly raises costs. Table 3.1 provides an overview of the described Java hardware.

Blank fields in the table indicate that the information is not available or not applicable (e.g. for simulation-only projects). Minimum CPI is the number of clock cycles for a simple instruction such as nop. One entry, the TINI system, is not a real Java hardware, but is included in the table since it is often incorrectly[1] cited as an embedded Java processor.

3.1 Hardware Translation and Coprocessors

The simplest enhancement for Java is a translation unit, which substitutes the switch statement of an interpreter JVM (bytecode decoding) through hardware and/or translates simple bytecodes to a sequence of RISC instructions on the fly.

A standard JVM interpreter contains a loop with a large switch statement that decodes the bytecode (see Listing 2.1). This switch statement is compiled to an indirect branch. The destinations of these indirect branches change frequently and do not benefit from branch-prediction logic. This is the main overhead for simple bytecodes on modern processors. The following approaches enhance the execution of Java programs on a standard processor through the substitution of the memory read and switch statement with bytecode fetch and decode through hardware.

---

[1] TINI is a standard interpreting JVM running on an enhanced 8051 processor.
[2] J2ME CLDC stands for Java2 Micro Edition, Connected Limited Device Configuration, which is described in Section 4.3.1.

	Type	Target technology	Size	Speed [MHz]	Java standard	Min. CPI
Hard-Int	Translation	Simulation only				
DELFT	Translation	Simulation only				
JIFFY	Translation	Xilinx FPGA	3800 LCs, 1KB RAM			
Jazelle	Co-processor	ASIC 0.18μ	12K gates	200		
JSTAR	Co-processor	ASIC 0.18μ Softcore	30K gates + 7KB	104	J2ME CLDC^2	
TINI	Software JVM	Enhanced 8051 clone			Java 1.1 subset	
picoJava	Processor	No realization	128K gates + memory		Full	1
aJile	Processor	ASIC 0.25μ	25K gates + ROM	100	J2ME CLDC^2	
Cjip	Processor	ASIC 0.35μ	70K gates + ROM, RAM	67	J2ME CLDC^2	6
Ignite	Stack pro-cessor	Xilinx FPGA	9700 LCs			
Moon	Processor	Altera FPGA	3660 LCs, 4KB RAM			
Lightfoot	Processor	Xilinx FPGA	3400 LCs	40		
LavaCORE	Processor	Xilinx FPGA	3800 LCs 30K gates	20		
Komodo	Processor	Xilinx FPGA	2600 LCs	20	Subset: 50 bytecodes	4
FemtoJava	Processor	Altera Flex 10K	2000 LCs	4	Subset: 69 bytecodes, 16-bit ALU	3
JSM [12]	Processor	Xilinx FPGA		3.5	Java Card	

Table 3.1: Java hardware

3.1.1 Hard-Int

Radhakrichnan [80] proposes an additional architecture for a standard RISC processor to speed up a JVM interpreter. The architecture, called Hard-Int, is placed between the cache and instruction fetch of the RISC processor. Simple Java bytecodes are translated to a sequence of RISC instructions. For native RISC code, the unit is bypassed. This architecture implements the expensive switch statement of a typical interpreter in hardware. A simulation of a SPARC processor with four execution units shows a speedup by the factor of 2.6 over JDK 1.2 JIT with SPECjvm98. Since the architecture is only evaluated in a software simulation, the impact of the inserted hardware on the clock frequency of the RISC processor is unknown. No estimation of the additional hardware cost for the translation unit is given.

3.1.2 DELFT-JAVA Engine

In his thesis [32], Glossner describes a processor for multimedia applications in Java. A RISC processor is extended with DSP capabilities and Java specific instructions. This combination results in a very complex processor. Simple JVM instructions are dynamically translated to the DELFT instruction set. However, no explanation is given as to how this is done. A new register-addressing mode, indirect register addressing with auto increment or decrement, provides support for stack caching in the register file. The translation of JVM bytecode to the DELFT instruction set maps stack-based dependencies into pipeline dependencies. The author expects that these dependencies can be resolved with standard techniques such as register renaming and out-of-order execution. To accelerate dynamic linking a link translation buffer cache resolved entries from the constant pool.

The processor is validated through a C++ model. An experiment with a synthetic benchmark (vector multiplication) compared a stack machine with an ideal register machine. The ideal register machine performs register renaming and out-of-order execution on multiple execution units. The achieved speedup in this experiment was 2.7. The high-level simulation model is more a proof of concept and no estimation is given for the resources needed to implement this complex processor. Since only a restricted subset of the JVM was simulated, no Java applications could be used to estimate the expected speedup.

3.1.3 JIFFY

An interesting approach to enhance Java execution in embedded systems is presented in Acher's thesis [1]. He states that JIT-compilation in software is not possible on most embedded devices because of resource constraints. JIFFY, a JIT in an FPGA, is proposed as a solution to this problem. The compilation is done in the following steps:

The Java bytecode is translated into an intermediate language with three registers and a stack. The reduction to three registers is due to the fact that bytecodes are using a maximum of three stack operands, and it simplifies translation to CISC-architectures with a low register count. In the next step, this instruction sequence, which is still stack-based, is optimized. The main effect of this optimization is to transform stack-based operations into register-based operations. These optimized instructions in the intermediate language are translated to native instructions of the target architecture in the last step.

The quality of the generated code was tested with software versions of JIFFY for a CISC (80586) and a RISC (Alpha 21164) architecture. The resulting code is about 1.1 to 7.5 times faster than interpreting Java bytecode on the x86 architecture. The speedup is similar to Suns first JIT compiler (sunwjit in JDK 1.1). The compilation time is estimated to be 50 to 70 clock cycles for one bytecode. This is 10 times faster than the efficient CACAO JIT [53]. A first prototype implementation in an FPGA used 3800 LCs and 8KBits RAM (80 % of a Xilinx XC2S200).

3.1.4 Jazelle

Jazelle [3] is an extension of the ARM 32-bit RISC processor, similar to the Thumb state (a 16-bit mode for reduced memory consumption). The Jazelle coprocessor is integrated into the same chip as the ARM processor. The hardware bytecode decoder logic is implemented in less than 12K gates. It accelerates, according to ARM, some 95% of the executed bytecodes. 140 bytecodes are executed directly in hardware, while the remaining 94 are emulated by sequences of ARM instructions. This solution also uses code modification with *quick* instructions to substitute certain object-related instructions after link resolution. All Java bytecodes, including the emulated sequences, are re-startable to enable a fast interrupt response time.

A new ARM instruction puts the processor into Java state. Bytecodes are fetched and decoded in two stages, compared to a single stage in ARM state. Four registers of the ARM core are used to cache the top stack elements. Stack spill and fill is handled automatically by the hardware. Additional registers are reused for the Java stack pointer, the variable pointer, the constant pool pointer and locale variable 0 (the *this* pointer in methods). Keeping the complete state of the Java mode in ARM registers simplifies its integration into existing operating systems.

3.1.5 JSTAR, JA108

Nozomi's JA108 [14], previously known as JSTAR, Java coprocessor sits between the native processor and the memory subsystem. JA108 fetches Java bytecodes from memory and translates them into native microprocessor instructions. JA108 acts as a pass-through when the core processor's native instructions are being executed. The JA108 is targeted for use in mobile phones to increase performance of Java multimedia applications. The coprocessor is available as standalone package or with included memory and can be operated up to 104MHz. The resource usage for the JSTAR is known to be about 30K gates plus 45Kbits for the microcode.

3.1.6 A Co-Designed Virtual Machine

In his thesis [49], Kent proposes an interesting new form of Java coprocessor. He investigates hardware/software co-design for a JVM within the context of a desktop workstation. The execution of the JVM is partitioned between an FPGA and the host processor. An FPGA board with local memory is connected via the PCI bus to the host. This solution provides an add-on accelerator without changing the system. Moreover, as the FPGA can be configured for a different task, the add-on hardware can be used for non-Java applications.

The critical issue in this approach is the partitioning of the JVM and the memory regions between hardware and software. Not all Java bytecodes can be executed in hardware. All object-oriented bytecodes are performed in software. However, once these bytecodes are replaced by their *quick* variants, some of them can then be executed in hardware. The most accessed data structures, i.e. the method's bytecode, execution stack and local variables, are placed in the FPGA board memory. The constant pool and the heap reside in the PC's main memory. The software part of the JVM decides during runtime which instruction sequences can be executed by the hardware. Due to the high cost of a context switch, this is a critical decision. Kent explored various algorithms with different block sizes to find the optimum partitioning of the instructions between the host processor and the FPGA. Tests with small benchmarks on a simulation showed performance gains by a factor of 6 to 11, when compared with an interpreting JVM. Kent is now working on the concurrent use of the FPGA and the host system to execute Java applications. Additional performance increases are expected for multi-threaded applications.

In our view, there are two potential problems with this approach. Firstly, the execution context for the hardware is too small. As invokevirtual and the quick version are implemented in the software partition, the maximum context is one method body. As shown in Section 5.1.2, Java methods are usually small (about 30% are less than 9 bytes long), resulting in many context switches. The second issue is the raw speedup, without communication overhead, of the FPGA solution. This speedup is stated to be around of 10 times greater, with the same clock frequency. However, FPGA clock rate will never reach the clock rate of a general-purpose processor. With a meaningful design, such as a CPU, the clock rate of an FPGA is about 20 to 50 times lower. However, everyone who uses an FPGA as target technology for a processor design faces this problem. It is better not to try to compete against mainstream PC technology.

3.2 Java Processors

Java Processors are primarily used in an embedded system. In such a system, Java is the native programming language and all operating system related code, such as device drivers, are implemented in Java. Java processors are simple or extended stack architectures with an instruction set that resembles more or less the bytecodes from the JVM.

3.2.1 picoJava

Sun's picoJava is the Java processor most often cited in research papers. It is used as a reference for new Java processors and as the basis for research into improving various aspects of a Java processor. Ironically, this processor was never released as a product by Sun. After Sun decided to not produce picoJava in silicon, Sun licensed picoJava to Fujitsu, IBM, LG Semicon and NEC. However, these companies also did not produce a chip and Sun finally provided the full Verilog code under an open-source license.

Sun introduced the first version of picoJava [73] in 1997. The processor was targeted at the embedded systems market as a pure Java processor with restricted support of C. picoJava-I contains four pipeline stages. A redesign followed in 1999, known as picoJava-II. This is the version described below. picoJava-II is now freely available with a rich set of documentation [89, 90].

Simple Java bytecodes are directly implemented in hardware, most of them execute in one to three cycles. Other performance critical instructions, for instance invoking a method, are implemented in microcode. picoJava traps on the remaining complex instructions, such as creation of an object, and emulates this instruction. To access memory, internal registers and for cache management picoJava implements 115 extended instructions with 2-byte opcodes. These instructions are necessary to write system-level code to support the JVM.

Traps are generated on interrupts, exceptions and for instruction emulation. A trap is rather expensive and has a minimum overhead of 16 clock cycles:

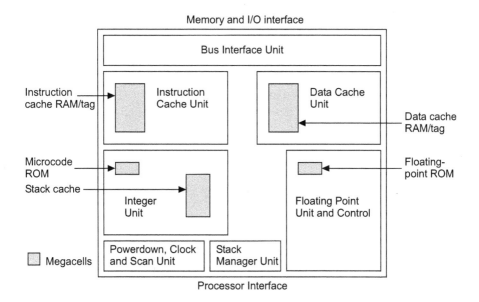

Figure 3.1: Block diagram of picoJava-II (from [89])

```
6 clocks trap execution
n clocks trap code
2 clocks set VARS register
8 clocks return from trap
```

This minimum value can only be achieved if the trap table entry is in the data cache and the first instruction of the trap routine is in the instruction cache. The worst-case interrupt latency is 926 clock cycles [90].

Figure 3.1 shows the major function units of picoJava. The integer unit decodes and executes picoJava instructions. The instruction cache is direct-mapped, while the data cache is two-way set-associative, both with a line size of 16 bytes. The caches can be configured between 0 and 16 Kbytes. An instruction buffer decouples the instruction cache from the decode unit. The FPU is organized as a microcode engine with a 32-bit datapath supporting single- and double-precision operations. Most single-precision operations require four cycles. Double-precision operations require four times the number of cycles as single-precision operations. For low-cost designs, the FPU can be removed and the core traps on floating-point instructions to a software routine to emulate these instructions. picoJava provides a 64-entry stack cache as a register file. The core manages this register file as a circular buffer, with a pointer to the top of stack. The stack management unit automatically performs spill

A Java instruction

```
c = a + b;
```

translates to the following bytecodes:

```
iload_1
iload_2
iadd
istore_3
```

Figure 3.2: A common folding pattern that is executed in a single cycle

to and fill from the data cache to avoid overflow and underflow of the stack buffer. To provide this functionality the register file contains five memory ports. Computation needs two read ports and one write port, the concurrent spill and fill operations the two additional read and write ports. The processor core consists of following six pipeline stages:

Fetch: Fetch 8 bytes from the instruction cache or 4 bytes from the bus interface to the 16-byte-deep prefetch buffer.

Decode: Group and precode instructions (up to 7 bytes) from the prefetch buffer. Instruction folding is performed on up to four bytecodes.

Register: Read up to two operands from the register file (stack cache).

Execute: Execute simple instructions in one cycle or microcode for multi-cycle instructions.

Cache: Access the data cache.

Writeback: Write the result back into the register file.

The integer unit together with the stack unit provides a mechanism, called instruction folding, to speed up common code patterns found in stack architectures, as shown in Figure 3.2. When all entries are contained in the stack cache, the picoJava core can fold these four instructions to one RISC-style single cycle operation.

picoJava contains a simple mechanism to speed-up the common case for monitor enter and exit. The two low order bits of an object reference are used to indicate the

lock holding or a request to a lock held by another thread. These bits are examined by
monitorenter and monitorexit. For all other operations on the reference, these
two bits are masked out by the hardware. Hardware registers cache up to two locks
held by a single thread.

To efficiently implement a generational or an incremental garbage collector picoJava offers hardware support for write barriers through memory segments. The
hardware checks all stores of an object reference if this reference points to a different
segment (compared to the store address). In this case, a trap is generated and the
garbage collector can take the appropriate action. Additional two reserved bits in the
object reference can be used for a write barrier trap.

The architecture of picoJava is a stack-based CISC processor implementing 341
different instructions [73] and is the most complex Java processor available. The
processor can be implemented [23] in about 440K gates (128K for the logic and
314K for the memory components: 284x80 bits microcode ROM, 2x192x64 bits
FPU ROM and 2x16KB caches).

3.2.2 aJile JEMCore

aJile's JEMCore is a direct-execution Java processor that is available as both an IP
core and a stand alone processor [2, 37]. It is based on the 32-bit JEM2 Java chip developed by Rockwell-Collins. JEM2 is an enhanced version of JEM1, created in 1997
by the Rockwell-Collins Advanced Architecture Microprocessor group. Rockwell-
Collins originally developed JEM for avionics applications by adapting an existing
design for a stack-based embedded processor. Rockwell-Collins decided not to sell
the chip on the open market. Instead, it licensed the design exclusively to aJile Systems Inc., which was founded in 1999 by engineers from Rockwell-Collins, Centaur
Technologies, Sun Microsystems, and IDT.

The core contains 24 32-bit wide registers. Six of them are used to cache the top
elements of the stack. The datapath consists of a 32-bit ALU, a 32-bit barrel shifter
and the support for floating point operations (disassembly/assembly, overflow and
NaN detection). The control store is a 4K by 56 ROM to hold the microcode that
implements the Java bytecode. An additional RAM control store can be used for
custom instructions. This feature is used to implement the basic synchronization and
thread scheduling routines in microcode. This results in low execution overheads
with thread-to-thread yield of less than one μs (at 100MHz). An optional Multiple
JVM Manager (MJM) supports two independent, memory protected JVMs. The two
JVMs execute time-sliced on the processor. According to aJile, the processor can be
implemented in 25K gates (without the microcode ROM). The MJM needs additional
10K gates.

Two silicon versions of JEM exist today: the aJ-80 and the aJ-100. Both versions comprise a JEM2 core, the MJM, 48KB zero wait state RAM and peripheral components, such as timer and UART. 16KB of the RAM is used for the writable control store. The remaining 32KB is used for storage of the processor stack. The aJ-100 provides a generic 8-bit, 16-bit or 32-bit external bus interface, while the aJ-80 only provides an 8-bit interface. The aJ-100 can be clocked up to 100MHz and the aJ-80 up to 66MHz. The power consumption is about 1mW per MHz.

Since aJile was a member of the Real-Time for Java Expert Group, the complete RTSJ will be available in the near future. One nice feature of this processor is its availability. A relatively cheap development system, the JStamp [91], was used to compare this processor with JOP.

3.2.3 Cjip

The Cjip processor [36, 43] supports multiple instruction sets, allowing Java, C, C++ and assembler to coexist. Internally, the Cjip uses 72 bit wide microcode instructions, to support the different instruction sets. At its core, Cjip is a 16-bit CISC architecture with on-chip 36KB ROM and 18KB RAM for fixed and loadable microcode. Another 1KB RAM is used for eight independent register banks, string buffer and two stack caches. Cjip is implemented in 0.35-micron technology and can be clocked up to 66MHz. The logic core consumes about 20% of the 1.4-million-transistor chip. The Cjip has 40 program controlled I/O pins, a high-speed 8 bit I/O bus with hardware DMA and an 8/16 bit DRAM interface.

The JVM is implemented largely in microcode (about 88% of the Java bytecodes). Java thread scheduling and garbage collection are implemented as processes in microcode. Microcode is also used to implement virtual peripherals such as watchdog timers, display and keyboard interfaces, sound generators and multimedia codecs.

Microcode instructions execute in two or three cycles. A JVM bytecode requires several microcode instructions. The Cjip Java instruction set and the extensions are described in detail in [42]. For example: a bytecode nop executes in 6 cycles while an iadd takes 12 cycles. Conditional bytecode branches are executed in 33 to 36 cycles. Object oriented instructions such as getfield, putfield or invokevirtual are not part of the instruction set.

3.2.4 Ignite, PSC1000

The PSC1000 [77] is a stack processor, based on ShBoom (originally designed by Chuck Moore [68]), designed for high speed Forth applications. The PSC1000 was later renamed to Ignite and promoted as a Java-processor, though it has it roots in

Forth. The instruction set, called ROSC (Removed Operand Set Computer), is different from Java bytecodes. A small JVM driver converts Java bytecode into the stack instruction set of the processor.

The processor contains two on-chip stacks, as usual in Forth processors [52], and additional 16 global registers. The first elements of the stacks are directly accessible. The bottleneck of instruction fetching without a cache is avoided by fetching up to four 8-bit instructions from a 32-bit memory. To simplify instruction decoding immediate values and branch offsets are placed right aligned in such an instruction group. The PSC1000 is available as ASIC at 80MHz and as a soft-core for Xilinx FPGAs (9700 LCs).

3.2.5 Moon

Vulcan ASIC's Moon processor is an implementation of the JVM to run in an FPGA. The execution model is the often-used mix of direct, microcode and trapped execution. As described in [63], a simple stack folding is implemented in order to reduce five memory cycles to three for instruction sequences like *push-push-add*. The first version of Moon uses 3.840 LCs and 10 embedded memory blocks in an Altera FPGA. The Moon2 processor [64] is available as an encrypted HDL source for Altera FPGAs (22% of an APEX 20K400E equates to 3660 LCs) or as VHDL or Verilog source code. The minimum silicon cost is given as 27K gates plus 3KB ROM and 1KB single port RAM. The single port RAM is used to implement 256 entries of the stack.

3.2.6 Lightfoot

The Lightfoot 32-bit core [62] is a hybrid 8/32-bit processor based on the Harvard architecture. Program memory is 8 bits wide and data memory is 32 bits wide. The core contains a 3-stage pipeline with an integer ALU, a barrel shifter and a 2-bit multiply step unit. There are two different stacks with top elements implemented as registers and memory extension. The data stack is used to hold temporary data – it is not used to implement the JVM stack frame. As the name implies, the return stack holds return addresses for subroutines and it can be used as an auxiliary stack. The TOS element is also used to access memory. The processor architecture specifies three different instruction formats: soft bytecodes, non-returnable instructions and single-byte instructions that can be folded with a return instruction. Soft bytecode instructions cause the processor to branch to one of 128 locations in low program memory, where the implementation of the soft bytecodes resides. This operation has a single cycle overhead and the address of the following instruction is pushed onto the return stack. The instruction set implies that it is optimized to write an efficient interpreted JVM.

The core is available in VHDL and can be implemented in less than 30K gates. According to DCT, the performance is typically 8 times better than RISC interpreters running at the same clock speed. The core is also provided as an EDIF netlist for dedicated Xilinx devices. It needs 1710 CLBs (= 3400 LCs) and 2 Block RAMs. In a Vertex-II (2V1000-5), it can be clocked up to 40MHz.

3.2.7 LavaCORE

LavaCORE [44] is another Java processor targeted at Xilinx FPGA architectures. It implements a set of instructions in hardware and firmware. Floating-point operations are not implemented. A 32x32-bit dual-ported RAM implements a register-file. For specialized embedded applications, a tool is provided to analyze which subset of the JVM instructions is used. The unused instructions can be omitted from the design. The core can be implemented in 1926 CLBs (= 3800 LCs) in a Virtex-II (2V1000-5) and runs at 20MHz.

3.2.8 Komodo

Komodo [95] is a multithreaded Java processor with a four-stage pipeline. It is intended as a basis for research on real-time scheduling on a multithreaded microcontroller [55]. Simple bytecodes are directly implemented, while more complex bytecodes, such as iaload, are implemented as a microcode sequence. The unique feature of Komodo is the instruction fetch unit with four independent program counters and status flags for four threads. A priority manager is responsible for hardware real-time scheduling and can select a new thread after each bytecode instruction.

The first version of Komodo in an FPGA implements a very restricted subset of the JVM (only 50 bytecodes). The design can be clocked at 20MHz. However, the pipeline runs at 5MHz for single cycle external memory access and three-port access of stack memory in one pipeline stage. The resource usage is 1300 CLBs (= 2600 LCs) in a Xilinix XC 4036 XL.

3.2.9 FemtoJava

FemtoJava [45] is a research project to build an application specific Java processor. The bytecode usage of the embedded application is analyzed and a customized version of FemtoJava is generated. FemtoJava implements up to 69 bytecode instructions for an 8 or 16 bit datapath. These instructions take 3, 4, 7 or 14 cycles to execute. Analysis of small applications (50 to 280 byte code) showed that between

22 and 69 distinct bytecodes are used. The resulting resource usage of the FPGA varies between 1000 and 2000 LCs. With the reduction of the datapath to 16 bits the processor is not Java conformant.

3.3 Additional Comments

The two classes of hardware accelerators for Java can be further subdivided as shown in Figure 3.3. Many of the Java processors are stack machines that have been derived from Forth processors. Two different stacks in these so-called Java processors (Cjip, Ignite and Lightfoot) do not fit very well for the JVM. Although stack based, Forth is different from Java bytecode. Instruction mix in Forth shows about 25% call and returns [52], so Forth processors are optimized for fast call and return. In Java, the percentage of call/return is only about 6% (see Section 5.1). With subroutine exits so common, it is no wonder that most of the Forth stack machines have a mechanism for combining subroutine exits with other instructions and provide two stacks to avoid the mixture of parameters and return addresses. However, a JVM stack frame is more complex than in Forth (see Section 5.5) and there is no use for such a mechanism. An additional return stack provides no advantage for the JVM.

In Forth only the top elements can be accessed, which results in a simple stack design with only one access port. In the JVM parameters for a method are explicitly pushed on the stack before invocation. These parameters are then accessed in the method relative to a variable pointer. This mechanism needs a dual ported memory with simultaneous read and write access. These basic differences between Forth and the JVM lead to a sub-optimal implementation of the JVM on a Forth based processor.

There are problems in getting information about commercial products. When new companies started developing Java processors, a lot of information was available. This information was usually more of a presentation of the concept, nevertheless it gave some insights into how they approached the different design problems. However, at the point at which the projects reached production quality, this information quietly disappeared from their websites. It was replaced with colorful marketing prospectuses about the wonderful world of the new Java-enabled mobile phones. Only one company, aJile Ltd., presented information about their product in a refereed conference paper.

Many research projects for a Java processor in an FPGA exists. Examples can be found in [45], [50] and [69]. These projects have much in common – the basic implementation of a stack machine with integer instructions is easy. However, the realization of the complete JVM is the hard part and therefore beyond the scope of these projects.

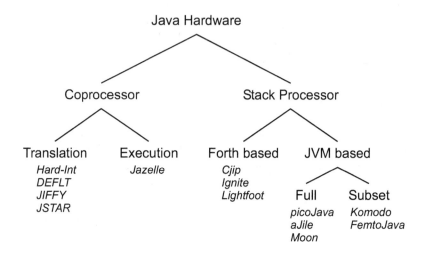

Figure 3.3: Java hardware

Other than the aJile processor and the Komodo project, no solution addresses the problem of real-time predictability. For this reason, as well as its availability, the aJile processor is used for comparison with JOP.

3.4 Research Objectives

In Table 3.2, features of selected Java processors are compared. Category 'Predictability' means how well the processor is time-predictable. In category 'Size', the chip size is estimated and category 'Performance' means average performance. The category 'JVM conformance' lists how complete the implementation of the JVM specification [60] is. The 'Flexibility' parameter indicates how well the processor can be adapted to different application domains.

The assessment of the various parameters is, however, somewhat subjective as the information is mainly derived from written documentation. In Section 7.3, the overall performance of various Java systems, including the aJile processor, is compared with JOP.

The last column of the table shows the features required for JOP. This is, therefore, our research objective in a nutshell.

Due to the great variation in execution times for a trap, picoJava is given a double minus in the 'Predictability' category. picoJava is also the largest processor in the list. However, its performance and JVM compatibility are expected to be superior to those of other processors.

	picoJava	aJile	Komodo	FemtoJava	JOP
Predictability	$--$	$\cdot$	$-$	$\cdot$	$++$
Size	$--$	$-$	$+$	$-$	$++$
Performance	$++$	$+$	$-$	$--$	$+$
JVM conformance	$++$	$+$	$-$	$--$	$\cdot$
Flexibility	$--$	$--$	$+$	$++$	$++$

Table 3.2: Feature comparison of selected Java processors

The aJile processor is intended as a solution for real-time systems. However, no information is available about bytecode execution times. As this processor is a commercial product and has been on the market for some time, it is expected that its JVM implementation would conform to Java standards, as defined by Sun.

Komodos multithreading is similar to hyper-threading in modern processors that are trying to hide latencies in instruction fetching. However, this feature leads to very pessimistic WCET values (in effect rendering the performance gain useless). The fact that the pipeline clock is only a quarter of the system clock also wastes a considerable amount of potential performance.

FemtoJava is given a double plus for flexibility, due to the application-dependent generation of the processor. However, FemtoJava is only a 16-bit processor and therefore not JVM compliant. The resource usage is also very high, compared to the minimal Java subset implemented and the low performance of the processor.

So far, all processors in the list perform weakly in the area of time-predictable execution of Java bytecodes. However, a low-level analysis of execution times is of primary importance for WCET analysis. Therefore, the main objective of this thesis is to define and implement a processor architecture that is as predictable as possible. However, it is equally important that this does not result in a low performance solution. Performance shall not suffer as a result of the time-predictable architecture.

The second main aim of this work is to design a small processor. Size and the resulting energy consumption are a main concern in embedded systems. The proposed Java processor needs to be small enough to be implemented in a low-cost FPGA device. With this constraint, an implementation in an ASIC will also result in a very small core that can be part of a larger system-on-a-chip.

The embedded market is diverse and one size does not fit all. A configurable processor in which we can trade size for performance provides the flexibility for a variety of application domains. The aim of the architecture of JOP is to support this flexibility.

As this thesis is more a technical than a theoretical study, the author believes that it is important to demonstrate the implementation of the proposed architecture. With a simulation, the ideas proposed cannot be verified to the extent necessary. Small details that are overlooked during simulation can render an idea impractical. Only a working version (ideally in a real-world project) of the processor can therefore provide the confidence that the above criteria are met.

The definition of Java does not work for hard real-time applications (described in detail in Chapter 4). In order to prove that JOP is a viable platform for real-time Java, part of this thesis looks at a definition of a real-time profile for Java.

The following list summarizes the research objectives for the proposed Java processor:

Primary Objectives:

- Time-predictable Java platform for embedded real-time systems

- Small design that fits into a low-cost FPGA

- A working processor, not merely a proposed architecture

Secondary Objectives:

- Acceptable performance compared with mainstream non real-time Java systems

- A flexible architecture that allows different configurations for different application domains

- Definition of a real-time profile for Java

4 Restrictions of Java for Embedded Real-Time Systems

Java was created as a part of the Green project specifically for an embedded device, a handheld wireless PDA. The device was never released as a product and Java was launched as the new language for the Internet. Over the time, Java got very popular to build desktop applications and web services. However, embedded systems are still programmed in C or C++. The pragmatic approach of Java to object orientation, the huge standard library and enhancements over C lead to a productivity increase, which now also attracts embedded system programmers. A built-in concurrency model and an elegant language construct to express synchronization between threads also simplify typical programming idioms in this area.

On the other hand, there are some issues with Java in an embedded system. Embedded systems are usually too small for JIT-compilation resulting in a slow interpreting execution model. Moreover, a major problem for embedded systems, which are usually also real-time systems, is the under specification of the scheduler. Even an implementation without preemption is allowed. The intention for this *loose* definition of the scheduler is to be able to implement the JVM on many platforms where no good multitasking support is available. The Real Time Specification for Java (RTSJ) [8] addresses many of these problems.

This section summarizes the issues with standard Java on embedded systems and describes various definitions for small devices given by Sun. It is followed by an overview of the two real-time extensions of Java and approaches for restricting the RTSJ for high-integrity applications. If, and how, these specifications are sufficient for small embedded systems in general and specifically for JOP is analyzed. The missing definition for small embedded real-time systems is provided in Section 6.1.

4.1 Java Support for Embedded Systems

When not using the cyclic executive approach, programming of embedded (real-time) systems is all about concurrent programming with time constraints. The basic functions can be summarized as:

- Threads

- Communication

- Activation

- Low level hardware access

Threads and Communication   Java has a built-in model for concurrency, the class `Thread`. All threads share the same heap resulting in a shared memory communication model. Mutual exclusion can be defined on methods or code blocks with the keyword `synchronized`. Synchronized methods acquire a lock on the object of the method. For synchronized code blocks, the object to be locked is explicitly stated.

Activation   Every object inherits the methods `wait()`, `notify()` and `notifyAll()` from `Object`. These methods in conjunction with synchronization on the object support activation.

     The classes `java.util.TimerTask` and `java.util.Timer` (since JDK 1.3) can be used to schedule tasks for future execution in a background thread.

4.2 Issues with Java in Embedded Systems

Although Java has language features that simplify concurrent programming the definition of these features is too vague for real-time systems.

Threads and Synchronization   Java, as described in [33], defines a very loose behavior of threads and scheduling. For example, the specification allows even low priority threads to preempt high priority threads. This protects threads from starvation in general purpose applications, but is not acceptable in real-time programming. Wakeup of a single thread with `notify()` is not precisely defined: *the choice is arbitrary and occurs at the discretion of the implementation.* It is not mandatory for a JVM to deal with the priority inversion problem.

     No notation of periodic activities, which are common in embedded systems programming, is available with the standard `Thread` class.

Garbage Collector   Garbage collection greatly simplifies programming and helps to avoid classic programming errors (e.g. memory leaks). Although real-time garbage collectors evolve, they are usually avoided in hard real-time systems. A more conservative approach to memory allocation is necessary.

WCET on Interfaces (OOP)   Method overriding and Interfaces, the simplified concept of multiple inheritance in Java, are the key concepts in Java to support object oriented programming. Like function pointers in C, the dynamic selection of the actual function at runtime complicates WCET analysis. Implementation of interface look up usually requires a search of the class hierarchy at runtime or very large dispatch tables.

Dynamic Class Loading   Dynamic class loading requires the resolution and verification of classes. This is a function that is usually too complex (and consumes too much memory) for embedded devices. An upper bound of execution time for this function is almost impossible to predict (or too large). This results in the complete avoidance of dynamic class loading in real-time systems.

Standard Library   For an implementation to be Java-conformant, it must include the full library (JDK). The JAR files for this library constitute about 15MB (in JDK 1.3, without native libraries), which is far too large for many embedded systems. Since Java was designed to be a safe language with a safe execution environment, no classes are defined for low-level access of hardware features. The standard library was not defined and coded with real-time applications in mind.

Execution Model   The first execution model for the JVM was an interpreter. The interpreter is now enhanced with Just-In-Time (JIT) compilation. Interpreting Java bytecodes is too slow and JIT compilation is not applicable in real-time systems. The time for the compilation process had to be included in the WCET, resulting in impracticable values.

Implementation Issues   The problems mentioned in this section are not *absolute* problems for real-time systems. However, they result in a slower execution model with a higher WCET.

According to [60] the static initializers of a class C are executed immediately before one of the following occurs: (i) an instance of C is created; (ii) a static method of C is invoked or (iii) a static field of C is used or assigned. The issue with this definition is that it is not allowed to invoke the static initializers at JVM startup and it is not so obvious when it gets invoked.

It follows that the bytecodes getstatic, putstatic, invokestatic and new can lead to class initialization and the possibility of high WCET values. In the JVM, it is necessary to check every execution of these bytecodes if the class is already

```
public class Problem {

    private static Abc a;
    public static int cnt; // implicitly set to 0

    static {
        // do some class initializaion
        a = new Abc();   //even this is ok.
    }

    public Problem() {
        ++cnt;
    }
}

// anywhere in some other class, in situation,
// when no instance of Problem has been created
// the following code can lead to
// the execution of the initializer
int nrOfProblems = Problem.cnt;
```

Listing 4.1: Class initialization can occur very late

initialized. This leads to a loss of performance and is violated in some existing implementations of the JVM. For example in CACAO [54] the static initializer is called at compilation time. Listing 4.1 shows an example of this problem.

Synchronization is possible with methods and on code blocks. Each object has a monitor associated with it and there are two different ways to gain and release ownership of a monitor. Bytecodes monitorenter and monitorexit explicitly handle synchronization. In other cases, synchronized methods are marked in the class file with the access flags. This means that all bytecodes for method invocation and return must check this access flag. This results in an unnecessary overhead on methods without synchronization. It would be preferable to encapsulate the bytecode of synchronized methods with bytecodes monitorenter and monitorexit. This solution is used in Suns picoJava-II [90]. The code is manipulated in the class loader. Two different ways of coding synchronization, in the bytecode stream and as access flags, are inconsistent.

4.3 Java Micro Edition

The definition of Java also includes the definition of the class library (JDK). This is a huge library[1] and too large for some systems. To compensate for this Sun has defined the *Java 2 Platform, Micro Edition* (J2ME) [66]. As Sun has changed the focus of Java targets several times, the specifications reflect this through their slightly chaotic manner. J2ME reduces the function of the JVM (e.g. no floating point support) to make implementation easier on smaller processors. It also reduces the library (API). J2ME defines three layers of software built upon the host operating system of the device:

Java Virtual Machine: This layer is just the JVM as in every Java implementation. Sun has assumed that the JVM will be implemented on top of a host operating system. There are no additional definitions for the J2ME in this layer.

Configuration: The configuration defines the minimum set of JVM features and Java class libraries available on a particular category of devices. In a way, a configuration defines the lowest common denominator of the Java platform features and libraries that the developers can assume to be available on all devices.

Profile: The profile defines the minimum set of Application Programming Interfaces (APIs) available on a particular family of devices. Profiles are implemented upon a particular configuration. Applications are written for a particular profile and are thus portable to any device that supports that profile. A device can support multiple profiles.

There is an overlap of the layers *configuration* and *profile*: Both define/restrict Java class libraries. Sun states: '*A profile is an additional way of specifying the subset of Java APIs, class libraries, and virtual machine features that targets a specific family of devices.*' However, in the current available definitions JVM features are only specified in *configurations*.

4.3.1 Connected Limited Device Configuration (CLDC)

CLDC is a configuration for connected devices with at least 192KB of total memory and a 16-bit or 32-bit processor. As the main target devices are cellular phones, this configuration has become very popular (Sun: '*CLDC was designed to meet the rigorous memory footprint requirements of cellular phones.*'). The CLDC is composed of the K Virtual Machine (KVM) and core class libraries. The following features have been removed from the Java language definition:

---

[1]In JDK 1.4 the main runtime library, rt.jar, is 25MB.

- Floating point support

- Finalization

Error handling has been altered so that the JVM halts in an implementation-specific manner. The following features have been removed from the JVM:

- Floating point support

- Java Native Interface (JNI)

- Reflection

- Finalization

- Weak references

- User-defined class loaders

- Thread groups and daemon threads

- Asynchronous exceptions

- Data type `long` is optional

These restrictions are defined in the final version 1.0 of CLDC. A newer version (1.1) again adds floating-point support. All currently available devices (as listed by Sun) support version 1.0.

The CLDC defines a subset of the following Java class libraries: `java.io`, `java.lang`, `java.lang.ref` and `java.util`. An additional library (`javax.microedition.io`) defines a simpler interface for communication than `java.io` and `java.net`. Examples of connections are: HTTP, datagrams, sockets and communication ports.

A small-footprint JVM, known as K Virtual Machine (KVM), is part of the CLDC distribution. KVM is suitable for 16/32-bit microprocessors with a total memory budget of about 128KB.

When implementing CLDC, one may choose to preload/prelink some classes. A utility (*JavaCodeCompact*) combines one or more Java class files and produces a C file that can be compiled and linked directly with the KVM.

There is only one profile defined under CLDC: the Mobile Information Device Profile (MIDP) defines a user interface for LC displays, a media player and a game API.

4.3.2 Connected Device Configuration (CDC)

The CDC defines a configuration for devices with network connection and assumes a minimum of a 32-bit processor and 2MB memory. CDC defines no restrictions for the JVM. A virtual machine, the CVM, is part of the distribution. The CVM expects the following functionality from the underlying OS:

- Threads

- Synchronization (mutexes and condition variables)

- Dynamic linking

- malloc (POSIX memory allocation utility) or equivalent

- Input/output (I/O) functions

- Berkeley Standard Distribution (BSD) sockets

- File system support

- Function libraries must be thread-safe. A thread blocking in a library should not block any other VM threads.

The tools *JavaCodeCompact* and *JavaMemberDepend* are part of the distribution. *JavaMemberDepend* generates lists of dependencies at the class member level. The existence of *JavaCodeCompact* implies that preloading of classes is allowed in CDC. Three profiles are defined for CDC:

Foundation Profile is a set of Java APIs that support resource-constrained devices without a standards-based GUI system. The basic class libraries from the Java standard edition (`java.io`, `java.lang` and `java.net`) are supported and a connection framework (`javax.microedition.io`) is added.

Personal Basis Profile is a set of Java APIs that support resource-constrained devices with a standards-based GUI framework based on lightweight components. It adds some parts of the Abstract Window Toolkit (AWT) support (relative to JDK 1.1 AWT).

Personal Profile completes the AWT libraries and includes support for the applet interface.

Although a device can support multiple profiles additional libraries for RMI and ODBC are known as *optional packages*.

4.3.3 Additional Specifications

The following specifications do not fit into the layer scheme of J2ME. However, they are defined in the same way as the above: subsets of the JVM and subsets/extensions of Java classes (API):

Java Card is a definition for the resource-constrained world of smart cards. The execution lifetime of the JVM is the lifetime of the card. The JVM is highly restricted (e.g. no threads, data type int is optional) and defines a different instructions set (i.e. new bytecodes to support smaller integer types).

Java Embedded Server is an API definition for services such as HTTP.

Personal Java was intended as a Java platform on Windows CE and is now marked as end of life.

Java TV is an extension to produce interactive television content and manage digital media. The description states that the JVM runs on top of an RTOS, but no real-time specific extensions are defined.

Other than Sun's, the few specifications that exist for embedded Java are:

leJOS [85] is a JVM for Lego Mindstorm with stronger restrictions on the core classes than the CLDC.

RTDA [87] although named 'Real-Time Data Access' the definition consists of two parts:

- An I/O data access API specification applicable for real-time and non real-time applications.
- A minimal set of real-time extensions to enable the I/O data access also to cover hard real-time capable response handling.

4.3.4 Discussion

Many of the specifications (i.e. *configurations* and *profiles*) are developed using the Java Community Process (JCP). JCP is not an open standard nor is it part of the open-source concept. Although the acronym J2ME implies Java version 2 (i.e. JDK 1.2 and later) almost all technologies under J2ME are still based on JDK 1.1.

Besides Java Card, CLDC is the 'smallest' definition from Sun. It assumes an operating system and is quite large (the JAR file for the classes is about 450KB). There are no API definitions for low-level hardware access. CLDC is not suitable for small embedded devices. Java Card defines a different JVM instruction set and thus compromises basic ideas of Java. A more restricted definition with following features is needed:

- JVM restrictions, such as in CLDC 1.0

- A package for low-level hardware access

- A minimum subset of core libraries

- Additional profiles for different application domains

4.4 Real-Time Extensions

In 1999, a document defining the requirements for real-time Java was published by NIST [47]. Based on these requirements, two groups defined specifications for real-time Java. A comparison of these two specifications and a comparison with Ada 95's Real-Time Annex can be found in [9]. The following section gives an overview of these specifications and additional defined restrictions of the RTSJ.

4.4.1 Real-Time Core Extension

The Real-Time Core Extension [86] is a specification published under the J Consortium. It is still in a draft version.

Two execution environments are defined: the *Core* environment is the special real-time component. It can be combined with a traditional JVM, the *Baseline*. For communication between these two domains, every Core object has two APIs, one for the Core domain and one for the Baseline domain. Baseline components can synchronize with Core components via semaphores.

Two forms of source code are supported to annotate attributes: *stylized* code with calls of static methods of special classes and *syntactic* code with new keywords. Syntactic code has to be processed by a special compiler or preprocessor.

Memory A new object hierarchy with `CoreObject` as root is introduced. To override final methods from `Object` the semantics of the class loader is changed. It replaces these methods with special named methods from `CoreObject`. A Core task is only allowed to allocate instances of `CoreObject` and its subclasses. These objects are allocated in a special allocation context or on the stack. The objects are not garbage collected. However, an allocation context can be explicit freed by the application.

Tasks and Asynchrony   Core tasks represent the analog of java.lang.Threads. All real-time tasks must extend CoreTask or one of its subclasses. No interface such as java.lang.Runnable is defined. Tasks are scheduled preemptive priority-based (128 levels) with FIFO order within priorities. Time slicing can be supported, but is not required.

Although stop() is depreciated in Java 2 it is allowed in the CoreTask for the asynchronous transfer of control (besides a class ATCEvent). To prevent the problem of inconsistent objects after stopping a task an *atomic synchronized* region defers abortion. A special task class is defined to implement interrupt service routines. The code for this handler is executed *atomically* and must be WCET analyzable. SporadicTask is used to implement responses to sporadic events, triggered by invoking the trigger() method of the task. No enforcement of a minimum time between arrivals of events is available. No special events or task types are defined for periodic work. The methods sleep() and sleepUntil() of CoreTask can be used to program periodic activities.

Exceptions   References from the java.lang.Throwable class hierarchy are silently replaced by the class loader with references to Core classes. A new scoped exception, which needs special support from the JVM, is defined.

Synchronization   Javas synchronized is only allowed on *this*. To compensate for this restriction additional synchronization objects such as semaphores and mutexes are defined. Queues on monitors, locks and semaphores are priority and FIFO ordered. Priority inversion is avoided by using the priority ceiling emulation protocol. To allow locks to be implemented without waiting queues, a Core task is not allowed to execute a blocking operation while it holds a lock.

Helper Classes   The standard representation of time is a long (64-bit) integer with nanosecond resolution. A Time class with static methods is provided for conversions. A helper class supports treating signed integers as unsigned values. Low-level hardware ports can be accessed via IOPort.

4.4.2 Discussion of the RT Core

A new introduced object hierarchy and new language keywords lead to changes in the class verifier and loader semantics. The behavior of the JVM has changed, so it would make sense to change the methods of Object to fit to the Core definition. This would result in a single object hierarchy. The restriction on synchronized disables the elegant style of expressing general synchronization problems in Java.

Although Nilsen lead the group, NewMonics PERC systems [71] supports a different API.

4.4.3 Real-Time Specification for Java

The Real-Time Specification for Java (RTSJ) defines a new API with support from the JVM [8]. The following guiding principles led to the definition:

- No restriction of the Java runtime environment

- Backward compatibility for non-real-time Java programs

- No syntactic extension to the Java language or new keywords

- Predictable execution

- Address current real-time system practice

- Allow future implementations to add advanced features

A Reference Implementation (RI) of the RTSJ forms part of the specification. The RTSJ is backward compatible with existing non-real-time Java programs, which implies that the RTSJ is intended to run on top of J2SE (and not on J2ME). The following section presents an overview of the RTSJ.

Threads and Scheduling   The behavior of the scheduler is clearer defined as in standard Java. A priority-based, preemptive scheduler with at least 28 real-time priorities is defined as base scheduler. Additional levels (ten) for the traditional Java threads need to be available. Threads with the same priority are queued in FIFO order. Additional schedulers (e.g. EDF) can be dynamically loaded. The class Scheduler and associated classes provide optional support for feasibility analysis.

Any instances of classes that implement the interface `Schedulable` are scheduled.   In the RTSJ `RealtimeThread`, `NoHeapRealtimeThread`, and `AsyncEventHandler` are *schedulable objects*.   `NoHeapRealtimeThread` has and `AsyncEventHandler` can have a priority higher than the garbage collector. As the available release-parameters indicate, threads are either periodic or bound to asynchronous events. Threads can be grouped together to bind the execution cost and deadline for a period.

Memory   As garbage collection is problematic in real-time applications, the RTSJ defines new memory areas:

Scoped memory is a memory area with bounded lifetime. When a scope is entered (with a new thread or through `enter()`), all new objects are allocated in this memory area. Scoped memory areas can be nested and shared among threads. On exit of the last thread from a scope, all finalizers of the allocated objects are invoked and the memory area is freed.

Physical memory is used to control allocation in memories with different access time.

Raw memory allows byte-level access to physical memory or memory-mapped I/O.

Immortal memory is a memory area shared between all threads without a garbage collector. All objects created in this memory area have the same lifetime as the application (a new definition of *immortal*).

Heap memory is the traditional garbage collected memory area.

Maximum memory usage and the maximum allocation rate per thread can be limited. Strict assignment rules between the different memory areas have to be checked by the implementation.

Synchronization   The implementation of `synchronized` has to include an algorithm to prevent priority inversion. The priority inheritance protocol is the default and the priority ceiling emulation protocol can be used on request. Threads waiting to enter a synchronized block are priority ordered and FIFO ordered within each priority. Wait free queues are provided for communication between instances of `java.lang.Thread` and `RealtimeThread`.

Time and Timers   Classes to represent relative and absolute time with nanosecond accuracy are defined. All time parameters are split to a `long` for milliseconds and an `int` for nanoseconds within those milliseconds. Each time object has an associated `Clock` object. Multiple clocks can represent different sources of time and resolution. This allows for the reduction of queue management overheads for tasks with different tolerance for jitter. A new type, rationale time, can be used to describe periods with a requested resolution over a longer period (i.e. allowing release jitter between the points of the *outer* period). Timer classes can generate time-triggered events (one shot and periodic).

Asynchrony Program logic representing external world events is scheduled and dispatched by the scheduler. An `AsyncEvent` object represents an external event (such as a POSIX signal or a hardware interrupt) or an internal event (through call of `fire()`). Event handlers are associated to these events and can be bound to a regular real-time thread or represent something *similar* to a thread. The relationship between events and handlers can be many-to-many. Release of handlers can be restricted to a minimum interarrival time.

Java's exception handling is extended to represent asynchronous transfer of control (ATC). `RealtimeThread` overloads `interrupt()` to generate an `AsynchronousInterruptedException` (AIE). The AIE is deferred until the execution of a method that is willing to accept an ATC. The method indicates this by including AIE in its throw clause. The semantics of `catch` is changed so that, even when it catches an AIE, the AIE is still propagated until the `happened()` method of the AIE is invoked. `Timed`, a subclass of AIE, simplifies the programming of timeouts.

Support for the RTSJ Implementations of the RTSJ are still rare and under development:

RI is the freely available reference implementation for a Linux system [93].

jRate is an open-source implementation [19] based on ahead-of-time compilation with the GNU compiler for Java.

FLEX is a compiler infrastructure for embedded systems developed at MIT [30]. Real-time Java is implemented with region-based memory management and a scheduler framework.

OVM is an open-source framework for Java [74]. The emphasis is on a JVM that is compliant with the RTSJ. RTSJ support is based on the translation of the complete Java application (including the library) to C and then compiling it into a native executable.

aJile will support the RTSJ with CLDC 1.0 on top of the aJ-80 and aJ-100 chips.

4.4.4 Discussion of the RTSJ

The RTSJ is a complex specification leading to a big memory footprint. The following list shows the size of the main components of the RI on Linux:

- Classes in javax/realtime: 343KB

- All classes in library foundation.jar: 2MB

- Timesys JVM executable: 2.6MB

The RTSJ assumes an RTOS and the RI runs on a heavyweight RT-Linux system. The RTSJ is too complex for low-end embedded systems. This complexity also hampers programming of high-integrity applications. The runtime memory allocation of the RTSJ classes has not been documented.

Threads and Scheduling   If a real-time thread is preempted by a higher priority thread, it is not defined if the preempted thread is placed in front or back of the waiting queue. It is not specified whether the default scheduler performs, or has to perform, time slicing between threads of equal priority.

Memory   It would be ideal if real-time systems were able to allocate all memory during the initialization phase and forbid dynamic memory allocation in the mission phase. However, this restricts many of Java's library functions.

The solution to this problem in the RTSJ is `ScopedMemory`, a memory space with limited lifetime. However, it can only be used as a parameter for thread creation or with `enter(Runnable r)`. In a system without dynamic thread creation, using scoped memory at creation time of the thread leads to the same behavior as using immortal memory.

The syntax with `enter()` leads to a cumbersome programming style: for each code part where limited lifetime memory is needed, a new class has to be defined and a single instance of this class allocated at initialization time. Trying to solve this problem elegantly with anonymous classes, as in Listing 4.2 (example from [10], p. 623), leads to an error.

On every call of `computation()`, an object of the anonymous class (and a `LTMemory` object) is allocated in immortal memory, leading to a memory leak. The correct usage of scoped memory is shown as a code fragment in Listing 4.3. The class `UseMem` only exists to execute the method `run()` in scoped memory. One instance of this class is created outside of the scoped memory.

A simpler[2] syntax is shown in Listing 4.4. The main drawback of this syntax is that the programmer is responsible for its correct usage.

New objects and arrays of objects have to be initialized to their default value after allocation [60]. This usually results in zeroing the memory at the JVM level and leads to variable (but linear) allocation time. This is the reason for the type `LTMemoryArea`

---

[2]This syntax is *not* part of the RTSJ. Is is a suggested change and part of the real-time profile defined in Section 6.1.

```
import javax.realtime.*;
public class ThreadCode implements Runnable
{
    private void computation()
    {
        final int min = 1*1024;
        final int max = 1*1024;
        final LTMemory myMem = new LTMemeory(min, max);
        myMem.enter(new Runnable()
        {
            public void run()
            {
                // access to temporary memory
            {
        } );
    }

    public void run()
    {
        ...
        computation();
        ...
    }
}
```

Listing 4.2: Scoped memory usage with a memory leak

```
class UseMem implements Runnable {

    public void run() {
        // inside scoped memory
        Integer[] = new Integer[100];
        ...
    }
}

// outside of scoped memory
// in immortal? at initialization?
LTMemory mem = new LTMemory(1024, 1024);
UseMem um = new UseMem();

// usage
computation() {
    mem.enter(um);
}
```

Listing 4.3: Correct usage of scoped memory in the RTSJ

```
LTMemory myMem;

// Create the memory object once
// in the constructor
MyThread() {
    myMem = new LTMemeory(min, max);
    ...
}

public void run() {
    ...
    myMem.enter();
    {   // A new code block disables access
        // to new objects in outer scope.
        // Access to temporary memory:
        Abc a = new Abc();
        ...
    }
    myMem.exit();
    ...
}
```

Listing 4.4: Simpler syntax for scoped memory

in the RTSJ. As suggested in [19], this initialization could be lumped together with the creation time and exit time of the scoped memory. This results in constant time for allocation (and usually faster zeroing of the memory).

With the RTSJ memory areas, it is difficult to move data from one area to another [70]. This results in a completely different programming model from that of standard Java. This can result in the programmer developing his/her own memory management.

Time and Timers   Why is the time split into milliseconds and nanoseconds? In the RI, it is converted to ns for add/subtract. After all mapping and converting (`AbsoluteTime`, `HighResolutionTime`, `Clock` and `RealTimeClock`) the `System.currentTimeMillis()` time, with a ms resolution, is used.

Since time triggered release of tasks can be modeled with periodic threads, the additional concept of timers is superfluous.

Asynchrony   An unbound `AsyncEventHandler` is not allowed to `enter()` a scoped memory. However, it is not clear if scoped memory is allowed as a parameter in the construction of a handler.

An unbound `AsyncEventHandler` leads to the implicit start of a thread on an event. This can (and, in the RI, does – see [19]) lead to substantial overheads. From the application perspective, bound and unbound event handlers behave in the same way. This is an implementation hint expressed through different classes. A consistent way to express the *importance* of events would be a scheduling parameter for the minimum allowed latency of the handler.

The syntax that is used in the throws clause of a method to state that ATC will be accepted is misleading. Exceptions in `throws` clauses of a method are usually *generated* in that method and not *accepted*.

J2SE Library   It is not specified which classes are safe to be used in `RealTimeThread` and `NoHeapRealTimeThread`. Several operating system functions can cause unbound blocking and their usage should be avoided. The memory allocation in standard JDK methods is not documented and their use in immortal memory context can lead to memory leaks.

Missing Features   There is no concept such as start mission. Changing scheduling parameters during runtime can lead to inconsistent scheduling behavior.

There is no provision for low-level blocking such as disabling interrupts. This is a common technique in device drivers where some hardware operations have to be atomic without affecting the priority level of the requesting thread (e.g. a low priority thread for a flash file system shall not get preempted during sector write as the chip internal write starts after a timeout).

On Small Systems   Many embedded systems are still built with 8 or 16-bit CPUs. 32-bit processors are seldom used. Java's default integer type is 32-bit, still large enough for almost all data types needed in embedded systems. The design decision in the RTSJ to use (often expensive) 64-bit `long` data is questionable.

4.4.5 Subsets of the RTSJ

The RTSJ is complex to implement and applications developed with the RTSJ are difficult to analyze (because of some of the sophisticated features of the RTSJ). Various profiles have been suggested for high-integrity real-time applications that result in restrictions of the RTSJ.

A Profile for High-Integrity Real-Time Java Programs

In [79], a subset of the RTSJ for the high-integrity application domain with hard real-time constraints is proposed. It is inspired by the Ravenscar profile for Ada [24] and focuses on exact temporal predictability.

Application structure: The application is divided in two different phases: *initialization* and *mission*. All non time-critical initialization, global object allocations, thread creation and startup are performed in the initialization phase. All classes need to be loaded and initialized in this phase. The mission phase starts after returning from `main()`, which is assumed to execute with maximum priority. The number of threads is fixed and the assigned priorities remain unchanged.

Threads: Two types of tasks are defined: *Periodic time-triggered activities* execute an infinite loop with at least one call of `waitForNextPeriod()`. *Sporadic activities* are modeled with a new class `SporadicEvent`. A `SporadicEvent` is bound to a thread and an external event on creation. Unbound event handlers are not allowed. It is not clear if the event can also be triggered by software (invocation of `fire()`). A restriction for a minimum interarrival time of events is not defined. Timers are not supported as time-triggered activities are well supported by periodic threads. Asynchronous transfers of control, overrun and miss handles and calls to `sleep()` are not allowed.

Concurrency: Synchronized methods with priority ceiling emulation protocol provide mutual exclusion to shared resources. Threads are dispatched in FIFO order within each priority level. Sporadic events are used instead of wait(), notify() and notifyAll() for signaling.

Memory: Since garbage collection is still not time-predictable, it is not supported. This implicitly converts the traditional heap to immortal memory. Scoped memory (LTMemory) is provided for object allocation during the mission phase. LTMemory has to be created during the initialization phase with initial size equal maximum size.

Implementation: For each thread and for the operations of the JVM the WCET must be computable. Code is restricted to bound loops and bound recursions. Annotations for WCET analysis are suggested. The JVM needs to check the timing of events and thread execution. It is not stated how the JVM should react to a timing error.

Ravenscar-Java

The Ravenscar-Java (RJ) profile [56] is a restricted subset of the RTSJ and is based on the work mentioned above. As the name implies it resembles Ravenscar Ada [24] concepts in Java.

To simplify the initialization phase, RJ defines Initializer, a class that has to be extended by the application class which contains main(). The use of time scoped memory is further restricted. LTMemory areas are not allowed to be nested nor shared between threads. Traditional Java threads are disallowed by changing the class java.lang.Thread. The same is true for all schedulable objects from the RTSJ. Two new classes are defined:

- PeriodicThread where run() gets called periodically, removing the loop construct with waitForNextPeriod().

- SporadicEventHandler binds a single thread with a single event. The event can be an interrupt or a software event.

Criticisms of Subsets of the RTSJ

If a new real-time profile is defined as a subset of the RTSJ it is harder for the programmer to find out which functions are available or not. This form of *compatibility* causes confusion. The use of different classes for a different specification is clearer and less error prone.

Ravenscar-Java, as a subset of the RTSJ, claims to be compatible with the RTSJ, in the sense that programs written according to the profile are valid RTSJ programs.

However, mandatory usages of new classes such as `PeriodicThread` need an emulation layer to run on an RTSJ system. In this case, it is better to define complete new classes for a subset and provide the mapping to the RTSJ. This allows a clearer distinction to be made between the two definitions.

It is not necessary to distinguish between heap and immortal memory. Without a garbage collector, the heap implicitly equals to immortal memory.

Objects are allocated in immortal memory in the initialization phase. In the mission phase, no objects should be allocated in immortal memory. Scoped memory can be entered and subsequent new objects are allocated in the scoped memory area. Since there are no circumstances in which allocation in these two memory areas are mixed, no `newInstance()` such as those in the RTSJ or Ravenscar-Java are necessary.

4.4.6 Extensions to the RTSJ

The Distributed Real-Time Specification for Java [46] extends RMI within the RTSJ. In 2000, it was accepted in the Sun Community Process as JSR-50. This specification is still under development. According to [94], three levels of integration between the RTSJ and RMI are defined:

Level 0: No changes in RMI and the RTSJ are necessary. The proxy thread on the server acts as an ordinary Java thread. Real-time threads cannot assume timely delivery of the RMI request.

Level 1: RMI is extended to Real-Time RMI. The server thread is a real-time thread that inherits scheduling parameters from the calling client.

Level 2: RMI and the RTSJ are extended to form the concept of *distributed real-time threads*. These threads have a unique system-wide identifier and can move freely in the distributed system.

4.5 Summary

In this section, we described definitions for embedded devices given by Sun. Most of these definitions are targeted for the mobile phone market and not for classical embedded systems.

Standard Java is under-specified for real-time systems. Two competing definitions, the 'Real-Time Core Extension' and the 'Real Time Specification for Java', address this problem. The RTSJ has been further restricted for high-integrity applications.

A similar definition that avoids inheritance of complex RTSJ classes is provided in Section 6.1.

5 JOP Architecture

This chapter presents the architecture for JOP and the motivation behind the various different design decisions we faced. First, we benchmark the JVM, in order to extract execution frequencies for the different bytecodes. These values will then guide the processor design.

Pipelined instruction processing calls for a high memory bandwidth. Caches are needed in order to avoid bottlenecks resulting from the main memory bandwidth. As seen in Chapter 2, there are two memory areas that are frequently accessed by the JVM: the stack and the method area. In this chapter, we will present time-predictable cache solutions for both areas.

5.1 Benchmarking the JVM

The rationale behind this section is best introduced with the warning from Computer Architecture: A Quantitative Approach [40] p. 63:

> Virtually every practicing computer architect knows Amdahl's Law. Despite this, we almost all occasionally fall into the trap of expending tremendous effort optimizing some aspect of a system before we measure its usage. Only when the overall speedup is unrewarding do we recall that we should have measured the usage of that feature before we spent so much effort enhancing it!

We measured how Java programs use the bytecode instruction set and explored the typical and worst-case method sizes. Our measurements and other reports are presented in the following sections.

5.1.1 Bytecode Frequency

The dynamic instruction frequency is the main measurement for determining a processor implementation. We can identify those instructions that should be fast. For seldom-used instructions, a trade-off can be made between performance and hardware resources.

Many reports have been written about JVM bytecode frequencies (e.g. [34, 81, 73]). Most of these reports provide only a coarse categorization of the bytecodes. For example, the bytecodes iload_n (load an int from a local variable) and getfield (fetch a field from an object) are combined in one instruction category. However, these instructions are very different in terms of their implementation complexity. We have chosen a fine-grained categorization of the bytecodes to gain greater insight into the bytecode usage. In Table 5.1 all 201 bytecode instructions are listed by category.

Three different applications were run on an instrumented JVM to measure dynamic bytecode frequency. The results were compared with the results from the above-mentioned reports. In Table 5.2 the dynamic instruction count for the three different benchmarks is shown. The last column is the average of the three tests weighted by the individual instructions count.

Kaffe [48] is an independent implementation of the JVM distributed under the GNU Public License. Kaffe was instrumented to collect data on dynamic bytecode usage. Three different applications were used as benchmarks to obtain the dynamic instruction count: JLex, KCJ and javac. JLex [6] is a lexical analyzer generator, written for Java in Java. The data was collected by running JLex with the provided sample.lex as the input file. KJC [31] is a Java compiler in Java, freely available under the terms of the GNU General Public License. javac is the Sun Java compiler. Both compilers were compiling part of the KJC sources during the benchmark. These benchmarks are similar to the benchmarks used in other reports and the results are therefore comparable. However, typical embedded applications can result in a slightly different instruction set usage pattern. Embedded applications are usually tightly connected with the environment and are therefore not available as stand-alone programs to serve as benchmark. An embedded application that was developed on JOP was adapted to serve as benchmark for Section 5.8 and Chapter 7.

In [25] the relationship between static and dynamic instruction frequency of 19 programs from the SPECjvm98 [17] and Java Grande benchmark suits were measured. The bytecodes categories were chosen different from the above measurements, but detailed enough to verify our own measurements. Table 5.3 shows the average dynamic execution frequency in percent[1] of selected bytecode categories from the SPEC and Java Grande benchmarks, compared with the results obtained by our measurements. The numbers in bold are categories or sums of categories that are comparable. The frequency of the load & const instructions is very similar to that in our measurements. However, field access, control instructions and method invocations are more frequent in our measurements. The higher count on field access instructions and method invocation can result from a more object oriented programming style in

---

[1] The values do not add up to 100% as only the most significant bytecode categories are shown

Type	Bytecode
load	aload, dload, fload, iload, lload
load (short)	aload_0, aload_1, aload_2, aload_3, dload_0, dload_1, dload_2, dload_3, fload_0, fload_1, fload_2, fload_3, iload_0, iload_1, iload_2, iload_3, lload_0, lload_1, lload_2, lload_3
store	astore, dstore, fstore, istore, lstore
store (short)	astore_0, astore_1, astore_2, astore_3, dstore_0, dstore_1, dstore_2, dstore_3, fstore_0, fstore_1, fstore_2, fstore_3, istore_0, istore_1, istore_2, istore_3, lstore_0, lstore_1, lstore_2, lstore_3
const	bipush, ldc, ldc_w, ldc2_w, sipush
const (short)	aconst_null, dconst_0, dconst_1, fconst_0, fconst_1, fconst_2, iconst_0, iconst_1, iconst_2, iconst_3, iconst_4, iconst_5, iconst_m1, lconst_0, lconst_1
get	getfield, getstatic
put	putfield, putstatic
alu	dadd, ddiv, dmul, dneg, drem, dsub, fadd, fdiv, fmul, fneg, frem, fsub, iadd, iand, idiv, imul, ineg, ior, irem, ishl, ishr, isub, iushr, ixor, ladd, land, ldiv, lmul, lneg, lor, lrem, lshl, lshr, lsub, lushr, lxor
iinc	iinc
stack	dup, dup_x1, dup_x2, dup2, dup2_x1, dup2_x2, pop, pop2, swap
array	aaload, aastore, baload, bastore, caload, castore, daload, dastore, faload, fastore, iaload, iastore, laload, lastore, saload, sastore
branch	goto, goto_w, if_acmpeq, if_acmpne, if_icmpeq, if_icmpge, if_icmpgt, if_icmple, if_icmplt, if_icmpne, ifeq, ifge, ifgt, ifle, iflt, ifne, ifnonnull, ifnull
compare	dcmpg, dcmpl, fcmpg, fcmpl, lcmp
switch	lookupswitch, tableswitch
call	invokeinterface, invokespecial, invokestatic, invokevirtual
return	areturn, dreturn, freturn, ireturn, lreturn, return
conversion	d2f, d2i, d2l, f2d, f2i, f2l, i2b, i2c, i2d, i2f, i2l, i2s, l2d, l2f, l2i
new	anewarray, multianewarray, new, newarray
other	arraylength, athrow, checkcast, instanceof, jsr, jsr_w, monitorenter, monitorexit, nop, ret, wide

Table 5.1: The 201 Java bytecodes and their assignment to different categories

	JLex	KJC	javac	Average
load (short)	32.72	31.45	27.24	30.37
get	12.02	14.39	17.04	15.04
branch	11.26	10.40	10.71	10.49
invoke	6.87	6.31	4.24	5.77
return	6.82	6.20	4.17	5.68
load	7.59	4.19	7.48	5.09
alu	2.60	4.43	4.74	4.48
const (short)	4.61	4.26	4.74	4.39
array	4.22	4.07	3.22	3.85
put	0.78	2.14	3.65	2.52
iinc	1.81	2.38	1.41	2.12
stack	1.30	2.11	2.11	2.10
store (short)	2.61	2.18	1.71	2.06
other	1.63	2.22	1.21	1.95
const	0.85	1.56	2.80	1.87
store	2.05	0.85	1.94	1.15
conversion	0.02	0.36	0.58	0.42
switch	0.00	0.20	0.60	0.30
new	0.08	0.28	0.20	0.25
compare	0.14	0.03	0.22	0.08

Table 5.2: Dynamic bytecode frequency in %

JLex, KJC and javac		SPEC and Java Grande	
Instruction	Frequency	Instruction	Frequency
load (short)	30.37	acnst	0.07
load	5.09	aload	16.23
const (short)	4.39	fcnst	0.33
const	1.87	fload	6.33
		icnst	3.21
		iload	18.06
load & const	**41.72**		**44.77**
get	15.04	field	11.12
put	2.52		
field access	**17.56**		**11.12**
branch	10.49	cjump	5.67
compare	0.08	ujump	0.51
control	**10.57**		**6.18**
invoke	**5.77**	**fcall**	**3.63**
return	**5.68**	retrn	**2.07**

Table 5.3: Dynamic bytecode frequency compared with the measurements from [25]

	virtual	special	static	interface
Java Grande	57.1	8.7	34.2	0.0
SPEC JVM98	81.0	10.9	2.9	5.2

Table 5.4: Types of different dynamic method calls for two benchmarks (from [76])

our selected applications than in the SPEC and Java Grande benchmarks. The big difference, not seen in our measurements, between the invoke and return frequency in the SPEC and Java Grande benchmarks is not explained in [25].

In all measurements, the load of local variables and constants onto the stack accounts for more than 40% of instructions executed. This feature shows that an efficient realization of the local variable memory area, the stack and the transfer between these memory areas is mandatory.

The next most executed bytecodes (`getfield` and `getstatic`) are the instructions that load an object or class field onto the operand stack. To account for these frequent instructions, the class layout for the runtime system has to be optimized for quick resolution of field addresses (i.e. minimum memory indirections).

The frequency of branches is comparable with the SPECint2000 measurements on RISC processors [40]. With such a high branch frequency, a processor without branch prediction logic is put under pressure in terms of pipeline length.

It is interesting to note that there are more method invoke instructions than return instructions. Two facts are responsible for this difference: native methods are invoked by a bytecode, but the return is inside the native methods; and an exception can result in a method exit without return.

5.1.2 Methods Types and Length

Table 5.4 shows the number of dynamic method calls of the Java Grande and SPECjvm98 benchmarks. It can be seen that the distribution of method types depends on the application type. Usage of virtual methods and interfaces is common in OO programming. Static methods result from the simple translation of procedural programs to Java.

As a basis for the proposed cache solution in Section 5.8, we will explore static distribution of method sizes. In the JVM, only relative branches are defined. The conditional branches and goto have an offset of 16 bits, resulting in a practical limit of the method length of 32KB. Although there is a goto instruction with a wide index (*goto_w*) that takes a 4-byte branch offset, other factors (e.g. indices in the exception table) limit the size of a method to 65535 bytes.

Length	Methods	Percentage	Cumulative percentage
1	1,388	1.94	1.94
2	1,580	2.21	4.16
4	1,871	2.62	6.78
8	16,192	22.67	29.45
16	12,363	17.31	46.76
32	12,638	17.70	64.45
64	11,178	15.65	80.10
128	7,287	10.20	90.31
256	4,304	6.03	96.33
512	1,727	2.42	98.75
1,024	592	0.83	99.58
2,048	175	0.25	99.83
4,096	75	0.11	99.93
8,192	37	0.05	99.98
16,384	11	0.02	100.00
32,768	1	0.00	100.00
65,536	0	0.00	100.00

Table 5.5: Static method count of different sizes from the runtime library (JDK 1.4).

Radhakrishnan et al. [81] measured the dynamic method size of the SPEC suit. They observed a 'tri-nodal' distribution, where most of the methods were 1, 9, or 26 bytecodes long. No explanation is given for the sizes of 9 or 26. The explanation of the 1 bytecode long methods as *wrapper methods* is wrong. For a wrapper method, the method needs to contain a minimum of two instructions (an invoke and a return). A single instruction method can *only* contain a return. However, this observation is in sharp contrast to the measurements obtained by Power and Waldron in [76].

In Table 5.5, the number of methods of different sizes in the Java runtime library (JDK 1.4) is shown. The library consists of 71419 methods, the largest being 16706 bytes. The size is classified by powers of 2 because we are interested in the size of cache memory for complete methods. In the table, the row of, for example, size 32 includes all methods of a size from 17 to 32 bytes. It can be seen that methods are typically very short. In fact, 99% of the methods are less than 513 bytes in size. This property is important for the proposed method cache in Section 5.8, where a complete method has to fit into the instruction cache.

All larger methods are different kinds of initialization functions, in most cases

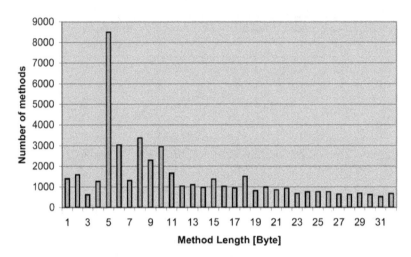

Figure 5.1: Static method count for methods of size up to 32 bytes in the JDK 1.4 runtime library. The horizontal axis indicates the method size.

<clinit>()[2]. The large class initialization methods typically result from the initialization of arrays with constant data. This is necessary because of the lack of initialized data segments, such as the BSS in C, in the Java class file. These initialization methods contain straight-line code and can therefore be split to smaller methods automatically, if necessary.

In Figure 5.1, the distribution of small methods up to a size of 32 bytes is shown. Figure 5.2 shows the method count for methods up to 300 bytes. As expected, we see fewer methods as size increases. We observed no surprise in the distribution, unlike the 'tri-nodal' distribution in [81]. The only method size that is very common is 5 bytes. These methods are the typical setter and getter methods in object-oriented programming as shown in Listing 5.1.

The method getVal() translates to three bytecodes of 1, 3 and 1 bytes in length respectively. These methods should show up in [81] as a peak at 3 bytecodes.

The static distribution of method sizes in an application (javac, the Java compiler) is quite similar to the distribution in the library. In the class file that contains the Java compiler, 98% of the methods are smaller than 513 bytes, and the larger methods are class initializers.

---

[2]The class or interface initialization method is static and the special name <clinit> is supplied by the compiler. These initialization methods are invoked implicitly by the JVM. The definition when these methods get invoked is problematic for the WCET analysis (see Section 4.2).

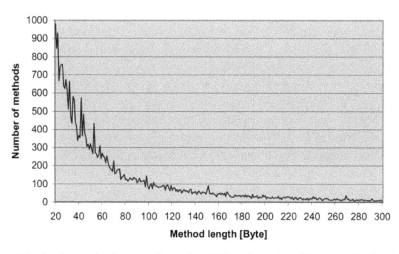

Figure 5.2: Static method count from the JDK 1.4 runtime library. The horizontal axis indicates the method size in bytes.

```
private int val;

public int getVal() {
    return val;
}

public int getVal();
Code:
0:   aload_0
1:   getfield         #2; //Field val:I
4:   ireturn
```

Listing 5.1: Bytecodes for a getter method

5.1.3 Summary

In this section, we performed dynamic measurements on the JVM instruction set. We saw that more than 40% of the executed instructions are local variables or constants loads onto the stack. This high frequency of stack access calls for an efficient implementation of the stack, as described in Section 5.5.

In addition, we have statically measured method sizes. Methods are typically very short. 30% of the methods are shorter than 9 bytes and 99% account for methods of up to 512 bytes. The maximum length is further limited by the definition of the class file. We will use this property in the proposed *method cache* in Section 5.8.

Instruction-usage data is an important input for the design of a processor architecture, as seen in the following sections.

5.2 Overview of JOP

This section gives an overview of JOP architecture. Figure 5.3 shows JOP's major function units. A typical configuration of JOP contains the processor core, a memory interface and a number of IO devices. The module extension provides the link between the processor core, and the memory and IO modules.

The processor core contains the four pipeline stages *bytecode fetch, microcode fetch, decode* and *execute*. The ports to the other modules are the address and data bus for the bytecode instructions, the two top elements of the stack (A and B), input to the top-of-stack (Data) and a number of control signals. There is no direct connection between the processor core and the external world.

The memory interface provides a connection between the main memory and the processor core. It also contains the bytecode cache. The extension module controls data read and write. The *busy* signal is used by the microcode instruction wait[3] to synchronize the processor core with the memory unit. The core reads bytecode instructions through dedicated buses (BC address and BC data) from the memory subsystem. The request for a method to be placed in the cache is performed through the extension module, but the cache hit detection and load is performed by the memory interface independently of the processor core (and therefore concurrently).

The I/O interface contains peripheral devices, such as the system time and timer interrupt, a serial interface and application-specific devices. Read and write to and

---

[3]The busy signal can also be used to stall the whole processor pipeline. This was the change made to JOP by Flavius Gruian [35]. However, in this synchronization mode, the concurrency between the memory access module and the main pipeline is lost.

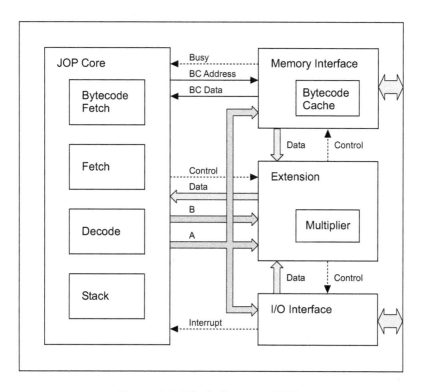

Figure 5.3: Block diagram of JOP

from this module are controlled by the extension module. All external devices[4] are connected to the I/O interface.

The extension module performs three functions: (a) it contains hardware accelerators (such as the multiplier unit in this example), (b) the control for the memory and the I/O module, and (c) the multiplexer for the read data that is loaded in the top-of-stack register. The write data from the top-of-stack (A) is connected directly to all modules.

The division of the processor into those four modules greatly simplifies the adaptation of JOP for different application domains or hardware platforms. Porting JOP to a new FPGA board usually results in changes in the memory module alone. Using the same board for different applications only involves making changes to the I/O module. JOP has been ported to several different FPGAs and prototyping boards and has been used in different applications (see Chapter 7), but it never proved necessary to change the processor core.

5.3 Microcode

The following discussion concerns two different instruction sets: *bytecode* and *microcode*. Bytecodes are the instructions that make up a compiled Java program. These instructions are executed by a Java virtual machine. The JVM does not assume any particular implementation technology. Microcode is the native instruction set for JOP. Bytecodes are translated, during their execution, into JOP microcode. Both instruction sets are designed for an extended[5] stack machine.

5.3.1 Translation of Bytecodes to Microcode

To date, no hardware implementation of the JVM exists that is capable of executing *all* bytecodes in hardware alone. This is due to the following: some bytecodes, such as new, which creates and initializes a new object, are too complex to implement in hardware. These bytecodes have to be emulated by software.

To build a self contained JVM without an underlying operating system, direct access to the memory and I/O devices is necessary. There are no bytecodes defined for low-level access. These low-level services are usually implemented in *native* functions, which means that another language (C) is native to the processor. However, for

---

[4]The external device can be as simple as a line driver for the serial interface that forms part of the interface module, or a complete bus interface, such as the ISA bus used to connect e.g. an Ethernet chip.

[5]An extended stack machine is one in which there are instructions available to access elements deeper down in the stack.

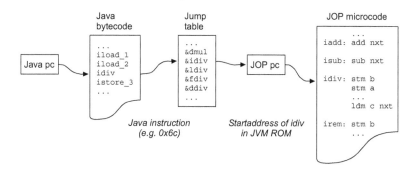

Figure 5.4: Data flow from the Java program counter to JOP microcode

a Java processor, bytecode is the *native* language.

One way to solve this problem is to implement simple bytecodes in hardware and to emulate the more complex and *native* functions in software with a different instruction set (sometimes called microcode). However, a processor with two different instruction sets results in a complex design.

Another common solution, used in Sun's picoJava [89], is to execute a subset of the bytecode native and to use a software trap to execute the remainder. This solution entails an overhead (a minimum of 16 cycles in picoJava, see 3.2.1) for the software trap.

In JOP, this problem is solved in a much simpler way. JOP has a single *native* instruction set, the so-called microcode. During execution, every Java bytecode is translated to either one, or a sequence of microcode instructions. This translation merely adds one pipeline stage to the core processor and results in no execution overheads. With this solution, we are free to define the JOP instruction set to map smoothly to the stack architecture of the JVM, and to find an instruction coding that can be implemented with minimal hardware.

Figure 5.4 gives an example of this data flow from the Java program counter to JOP microcode. The fetched bytecode acts as an index for the jump table. The jump table contains the start addresses for the JVM implementation in microcode. This address is loaded into the JOP program counter for every bytecode executed.

Every bytecode is translated to an address in the microcode that implements the JVM. If there exists an equivalent JOP instruction for the bytecode, it is executed in one cycle and the next bytecode is translated. For a more complex bytecode, JOP just continues to execute microcode in the subsequent cycles. The end of this sequence is coded in the microcode instruction (as the *nxt* bit).

5.3.2 Compact Microcode

For the JVM to be implemented efficiently, the microcode has to *fit* to the Java byte-code. Since the JVM is a stack machine, the microcode is also stack-oriented. However, the JVM is not a pure stack machine. Method parameters and local variables are defined as *locals*. These locals can reside in a stack frame of the method and are accessed with an offset relative to the start of this *locals* area.

Additional local variables (16) are available at the microcode level. These variables serve as scratch variables, like registers in a conventional CPU. However, arithmetic and logic operations are performed on the stack.

Some bytecodes, such as ALU operations and the short form access to *locals*, are directly implemented by an equivalent microcode instruction (with a different encoding). Additional instructions are available to access internal registers, main memory and I/O devices. A relative conditional branch (zero/non zero of TOS) performs control flow decisions at the microcode level. For optimum use of the available memory resources, all instructions are 8 bits long. There are no variable-length instructions and every instruction, with the exception of wait, is executed in a single cycle. To keep the instruction set this dense, two concepts are applied:

Two types of operands, immediate values and branch distances, normally force an instruction set to be longer than 8 bits. The instruction set is either expanded to 16 or 32 bits, as in typical RISC processors, or allowed to be of variable length at byte boundaries. A first implementation of the JVM with a 16-bit instruction set showed that only a small number of different constants are necessary for immediate values and relative branch distances.

In the current realization of JOP, the different immediate values are collected while the microcode is being assembled and are put into the initialization file for the local RAM. These constants are accessed indirectly in the same way as the local variables. They are similar to initialized variables, apart from the fact that there are no operations to change their value during runtime, which would serve no purpose and would waste instruction codes.

A similar solution is used for branch distances. The assembler generates a VHDL file with a table for all found branch constants. This table is indexed using instruction bits during runtime. These indirections during runtime make it possible to retain an 8-bit instruction set, and provide 16 different immediate values and 32 different branch constants. For a general purpose instruction set, these indirections would impose too many restrictions. As the microcode only implements the JVM, this solution is a viable option.

To simplify the logic for instruction decoding, the instruction coding is carefully chosen. For example, one bit in the instruction specifies whether the instruction will increment or decrement the stack pointer. The offset to access the *locals* is directly encoded in the instruction. This is not the case for the original encoding of the equivalent bytecodes (e.g. *iload_0* is 0x1a and *iload_1* is 0x1b). Whenever a multiplexer depends on an instruction, the selection is directly encoded in the instruction.

5.3.3 Instruction Set

JOP implements 43 different microcode instructions. These instructions are encoded in 8 bits. With the addition of the *nxt* and *opd* bits in every instruction, the effective instruction length is 10 bits.

Bytecode equivalent: These instructions are direct implementations of bytecodes and result in one cycle execution time for the bytecode (except st and ld): pop, and, or, xor, add, sub, st<n>, st, ushr, shl, shr, nop, ld<n>, ld, dup

Local memory access: The first 16 words in the internal stack memory are reserved for internal variables. The next 16 words contain constants. These memory locations are accessed using the following instructions: stm, ldm, ldi

Register manipulation: The stack pointer, the variable pointer and the Java program counter are loaded or stored with: stvp, stjpc, stsp, ldvp, ldjpc, ldsp

Bytecode operand: The operand is loaded from the bytecode RAM, converted to a 32-bit word and pushed on the stack with: ld_opd_8s, ld_opd_8u, ld_opd_16s, ld_opd_16u

External memory access: The autonomous memory subsystem is accessed using the following instructions: stmra, stmwa, stmwd, wait, ldmrd, stbcrd, ldbcstart

IO device access: The following instructions permit access to the IO subsystem: stioa, stiod, ldiod

Multiplier: The multiplier is accessed with: stmul, ldmul

Microcode branches: Two conditional branches in microcode are available: bz, bnz

Bytecode branch: All 17 bytecode branch instructions are mapped to one instruction: jbr

A detailed description of the microcode instructions can be found in Appendix C.

5.3.4 Bytecode Example

The example in Listing 5.2 shows the implementation of a single cycle bytecode and an infrequent bytecode as a sequence of JOP instructions. In this example, the dup bytecode is mapped to the equivalent dup microcode and executed in a single cycle, whereas dup_x1 takes five cycles to execute, and after the last instruction (ldm a nxt), the first instruction for the next bytecode is executed.

```
dup:    dup nxt     // 1 to 1 mapping


//  a and b are scratch variables for the
//  JVM code.
dup_x1: stm a       // save TOS
        stm b       // and TOS-1
        ldm a       // duplicate former TOS
        ldm b       // restore TOS-1
        ldm a nxt   // restore TOS and fetch next bytecode
```

Listing 5.2: Implementation of dup and dup_x1

Some bytecodes are followed by operands of between one and three bytes in length (except lookupswitch and tableswitch). Due to pipelining, the first operand byte that follows the bytecode instruction is available when the first microcode instruction enters the execution stage. If this is a one-byte long operand, it is ready to be accessed. The increment of the Java program counter after the read of an operand byte is coded in the JOP instruction (an *opd* bit similar to the *nxt* bit).

In Listing 5.3, the implementation of sipush is shown. The bytecode is followed by a two-byte operand. Since the access to bytecode memory is only one byte per cycle, *opd* and *nxt* are not allowed at the same time. This implies a minimum execution time of $n + 1$ cycles for a bytecode with n operand bytes.

```
sipush: nop opd         // fetch next byte
        nop opd         // and one more
        ld_opd_16s nxt  // load 16 bit operand
```

Listing 5.3: Bytecode operand load

5.3.5 Flexible Implementation of Bytecodes

As mentioned above, some Java bytecodes are very complex. One solution already described is to emulate them through a sequence of microcode instructions. However, some of the more complex bytecodes are very seldom used. To further reduce the resource implications for JOP, in this case local memory, bytecodes can even be implemented by *using* Java bytecodes. During the assembly of the JVM, all labels that represent an entry point for the bytecode implementation are used to generate the translation table. For all bytecodes for which no such label is found, i.e. there is no implementation in microcode, a *not-implemented* address is generated. The instruction sequence at this address invokes a static method from a system class (com.jopdesign.sys.JVM). This class contains 256 static methods, one for each possible bytecode, ordered by the bytecode value. The bytecode is used as the index in the method table of this system class. As described in Section 5.6, this feature also allows for the easy configuration of resource usage versus performance.

5.3.6 Summary

In order to handle the great variation in the complexity of Java bytecodes we have proposed a translation to a different instruction set, the so-called microcode. This microcode is still an instruction set for a stack machine, but more RISC-like than the CISC-like JVM bytecodes.

In the next section we will see how this translation is handled in JOP's pipeline and how it can simplify interrupt handling.

5.4 The Processor Pipeline

JOP is a fully pipelined architecture with single cycle execution of microcode instructions and a novel approach to mapping Java bytecode to these instructions. Figure 5.5 shows the datapath for JOP.

Three stages form the JOP core, executing microcode instructions. An additional stage in the front of the core pipeline fetches Java bytecodes – the instructions of the JVM – and translates these bytecodes into addresses in microcode. Bytecode branches are also decoded and executed in this stage. The second pipeline stage fetches JOP instructions from the internal microcode memory and executes microcode branches. Besides the usual decode function, the third pipeline stage also generates addresses for the stack RAM. As every stack machine instruction has either *pop* or *push* characteristics, it is possible to generate fill or spill addresses for the *following* instruction at this stage. The last pipeline stage performs ALU operations, load, store and stack spill or fill. At the execution stage, operations are performed with the two topmost elements of the stack.

The stack architecture allows for a short pipeline, which results in short branch delays. Two branch delay slots are available after a conditional microcode branch.

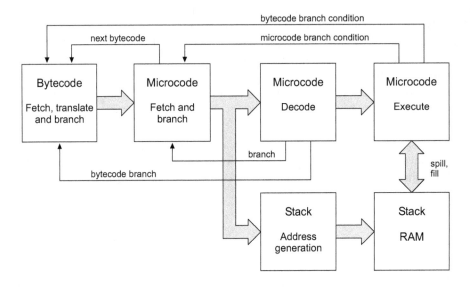

Figure 5.5: Datapath of JOP

The method cache (*Bytecode RAM*), microcode ROM, and stack RAM are implemented with single cycle access in the FPGA's internal memories.

5.4.1 Java Bytecode Fetch

In the first pipeline stage, as shown in Figure 5.6, the Java bytecodes are fetched from the internal memory (*Bytecode RAM*). The bytecode is mapped through the translation table into the address (*jpaddr*) for the microcode ROM.

The fetched bytecode results in an absolute jump in the microcode (the second stage). If the bytecode is mapped one-to-one with a JOP instruction, the following fetched bytecode again results in a jump in the microcode in the following cycle. If the bytecode is a complex one, JOP continues to execute microcode. At the end of this instruction sequence the next bytecode, and therefore the new jump address, is requested (signal *nxt*).

The bytecode RAM serves as instruction cache and is filled on method invoke and return. Details about this time-predictable instruction cache can be found in Section 5.8.

The bytecode is also stored in a register for later use as an operand (requested by signal *opd*). Bytecode branches are also decoded and executed in this stage. Since *jpc* is also used to read the operands, the program counter is saved in *jpcbr* during an instruction fetch. *jinstr* is used to decode the branch type and *jpcbr* to calculate the

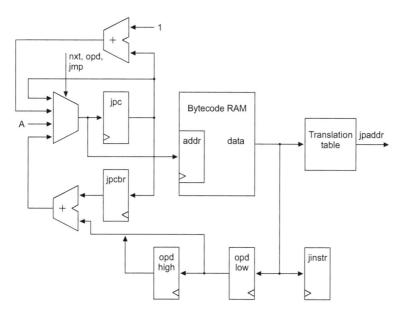

Figure 5.6: Java bytecode fetch

branch target address.

5.4.2 JOP Instruction Fetch

The second pipeline stage, as shown in Figure 5.7, fetches JOP instructions from the internal microcode memory and executes microcode branches.

The JOP microcode, which implements the JVM, is stored in the microcode ROM. The program counter pc is incremented during normal execution. If the instruction is labeled with *nxt* a new bytecode is requested from the first stage and pc is loaded with *jpaddr*. *jpaddr* is the starting address for the implementation of that bytecode. The label *nxt* is the flag that marks the end of the microcode instruction stream for one bytecode. Another flag, *opd*, indicates that a bytecode operand needs to be fetched in the first pipeline stage. Both flags are stored in a table that is indexed by the program counter.

brdly contains the target address for a conditional branch. The same offset is shared by a number of branch destinations. A table (*branch offset*) is used to store these relative offsets. This indirection means that only 5 bits need to be used in the instruction coding for branch targets and thereby allow greater offsets. The three tables *BC fetch table*, *branch offset* and *translation table* (from the bytecode fetch stage) are gener-

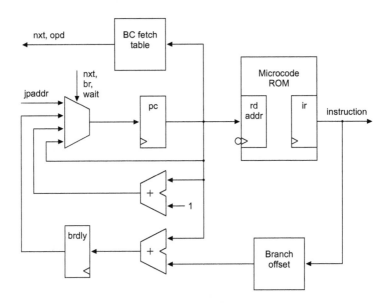

Figure 5.7: JOP instruction fetch

ated during the assembly of the JVM code. The outputs are plain VHDL files. For an implementation in an FPGA, recompiling the design after changing the JVM implementation is a straightforward operation. For an ASIC with a loadable JVM, it is necessary to implement a different solution.

FPGAs available to date do not allow asynchronous memory access. They therefore force us to use the registers in the memory blocks. However, the output of these registers is not accessible. To avoid having to create an additional pipeline stage just for a register-register move, the read address register of the microcode ROM is clocked on the negative edge.

An alternative solution for this problem would be to use the output of the multiplexer for the *pc* and the read address register of the memory. However, this solution results in a longer critical path, as the multiplexer can no longer be combined with the flip-flops that form the *pc* in the same LCs. This is an example of how implementation technology (the FPGA) can influence the architecture.

5.4.3 Decode and Address Generation

Besides the usual decode function, the third pipeline, as shown in Figure 5.8, also generates addresses for the stack RAM.

As we can see in Section 5.5 Table 5.10, read and write addresses are either relative

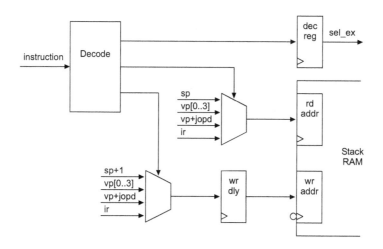

Figure 5.8: Decode and address generation

to the stack pointer or to the variable pointer. The selection of the pre-calculated address can be performed in the decode stage. When an address relative to the stack pointer is used (either as read or as write address, never for both) the stack pointer is also decremented or incremented in the decode stage.

Stack machine instructions can be categorized from a stack manipulation perspective as either *pop* or *push*. This allows us to generate fill or spill TOS-1 addresses for the *following* instruction during the decode stage, thereby saving one extra pipeline stage.

5.4.4 Execute

At the execution stage, as shown in Figure 5.9, operations are performed using two discrete registers: TOS and TOS-1, labeled *A* and *B*.

Each arithmetic/logical operation is performed with registers *A* and *B* as the source, and register *A* as the destination. All load operations (local variables, internal register, external memory and periphery) result in a value being loaded into register *A*. There is therefore no need for a write-back pipeline stage. Register *A* is also the source for the store operations. Register *B* is never accessed directly. It is read as an implicit operand or for stack spill on push instructions. It is written during the stack spill with the content of the stack RAM or the stack fill with the content of register *A*.

Beside the Java stack, the stack RAM also contains microcode variables and constants. This resource-sharing arrangement not only reduces the number of memory blocks needed for the processor, but also the number of data paths to and from the

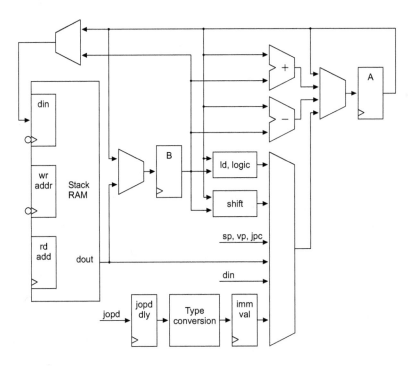

Figure 5.9: Execution stage

register A.

The inverted clock on data-in and on the write address register of the stack RAM is used, for the same reason, as on the read address register of the microcode ROM.

A stack machine with two explicit registers for the two topmost stack elements and automatic fill/spill needs neither an extra write-back stage nor any data forwarding. Details of this two-level stack architecture are described in Section 5.5.

5.4.5 Interrupt Logic

Interrupts are considered hard to handle in a pipelined processor, meaning implementation tends to be complex (and therefore resource consuming). In JOP, the bytecode-microcode translation is used cleverly to avoid having to handle interrupts in the core pipeline.

Interrupts are implemented as special bytecodes. These bytecodes are inserted by the hardware in the Java instruction stream. When an interrupt is pending and the next fetched byte from the bytecode RAM is an instruction (as indicated by the *nxt* bit in the microcode), the associated special bytecode is used instead of the instruction from the bytecode RAM. The result is that interrupts are accepted at bytecode boundaries. The worst-case preemption delay is the execution time of the *slowest* bytecode that is implemented in microcode. Bytecodes that are implemented in Java can be interrupted.

The implementation of interrupts at the bytecode-microcode mapping stage keeps interrupts transparent in the core pipeline and avoids complex logic. Interrupt handlers can be implemented in the same way as standard bytecodes are implemented i.e. in microcode or Java.

This special bytecode can result in a call of a JVM internal method in the context of the interrupted thread. This mechanism implicitly stores almost the complete context of the current active thread on the stack.

5.4.6 Summary

In this section, we have analyzed JOP's pipeline. The core of the stack machine constitutes a three-stage pipeline. In the following section, we will see that this organization is an optimal solution for the stack access pattern of the JVM.

An additional pipeline stage in front of this core pipeline stage performs bytecode fetch and the translation to microcode. This organization has zero overheads for more complex bytecodes and results in the short pipeline that is necessary for any processor without branch prediction. This additional translation stage also presents an elegant way of incorporating interrupts virtually *for free*.

5.5 An Efficient Stack Machine

The concept of a stack has a long tradition, but stack machines no longer form part of mainstream computers. Although stacks are no longer used for expression evaluation, they are still used for the context save on a function call. A niche language, Forth [52], is stack-based and known as an efficient language for controller applications. Some hardware implementations of the Forth abstract machine do exist. These Forth processors are stack machines.

The Java programming language defines not only the language but also a binary representation of the program and an abstract machine, the JVM, to execute this binary. The JVM is similar to the Forth abstract machine in that it is also a stack machine. However, the usage of the stack differs from Forth in such a way that a Forth processor is not an ideal hardware platform to execute Java programs.

In this section, the stack usage in the JVM is analyzed. We will see that, besides the access to the top elements of the stack, an additional access path to an arbitrary element of the stack is necessary for an efficient implementation of the JVM. Two architectures will be presented for this mixed access mode of the stack. Both architectures are used in Java processors. However, we will also show that the JVM does not need a full three-port access to the stack as implemented in the two architectures. This allows for a simple and more elegant design of the stack for a Java processor. This proposed architecture will then be compared with the other two at the end of this section.

5.5.1 Java Computing Model

The JVM is not a pure stack machine in the sense of, for instance, the stack model in Forth. The JVM operates on a LIFO stack as its *operand stack*. The JVM supplies instructions to load values on the operand stack, and other instructions take their operands from the stack, operate on them and push the result back onto the stack. For example, the iadd instruction pops two values from the stack and pushes the result back onto the stack. These instructions are the stack machine's typical zero-address instructions. The maximum depth of this operand stack is known at compile time. In typical Java programs, the maximum depth is very small. To illustrate the operation notation of the JVM, Table 5.6 shows the evaluation of an expression for a stack machine notation and the JVM bytecodes. Instruction iload_n loads an integer value from a local variable at position n and pushes the value on TOS.

The JVM contains another memory area for method local data. This area is known as *local variables*. Primitive type values, such as integer and float, and references to objects are stored in these local variables. Arrays and objects cannot be allocated

$A = B + C * D$	
Stack	JVM
push B	iload_1
push C	iload_2
push D	iload_3
*	imul
+	iadd
pop A	istore_0

Table 5.6: Standard stack notation and the corresponding JVM instructions

in a local variable, as in C/C++. They have to be placed on the heap. Different instructions transfer data between the operand stack and the local variables. Access to the first four elements is optimized with dedicated single byte instructions, while up to 256 local variables are accessed with a two-byte instruction and, with the wide modifier, the area can contain up to 65536 values.

These local variables are very similar to registers and it appears that some of these locals can be mapped to the registers of a general purpose CPU or implemented as registers in a Java processor. On method invocation, local variables could be saved in a frame on a stack, different from the operand stack, together with the return address, in much the same way as in C on a typical processor. This would result in the following memory hierarchy:

- On-chip hardware stack for ALU operations

- A small register file for frequently-accessed variables

- A method stack in main memory containing the return address and additional local variables

However, the semantics of method invocation suggest a different model. The arguments of a method are pushed on the operand stack. In the invoked method, these arguments are not on the operand stack but are instead accessed as the first variables in the local variable area. The *real* method local variables are placed at higher indices. Listing 5.4 gives an example of the argument passing mechanism in the JVM. These arguments could be copied to the local variable area of the invoked method. To avoid this memory transfer, the entire variable area (the arguments *and* the variables of the method) is allocated on the operand stack. However, in the invoked method, the arguments are buried deep in the stack.

The Java source:

```
int val = foo(1, 2);
...
public int foo(int a, int b) {
    int c = 1;
    return a+b+c;
}
```

Compiled bytecode instructions for the JVM:

The invocation sequence:
```
aload_0              // Push the object reference
iconst_1             // and the parameter onto the
iconst_2             // operand stack.
invokevirtual   #2   // Invoke method foo:(II)I.
istore_1             // Store the result in val.
```

public int foo(int,int):
```
iconst_1             // The constant is stored in a method
istore_3             // local variable (at position 3).
iload_1              // Arguments are accessed as locals
iload_2              // and pushed onto the operand stack.
iadd                 // Operation on the operand stack.
iload_3              // Push c onto the operand stack.
iadd
ireturn              // Return value is on top of stack.
```

Listing 5.4: Example of parameter passing and access

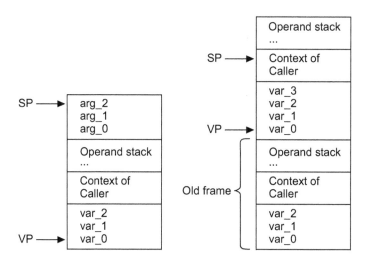

Figure 5.10: Stack change on method invocation

This asymmetry in the argument handling prohibits passing down parameters through multiple levels of subroutine calls, as in Forth. Therefore, an extra stack for return addresses is of no use for the JVM. This single stack now contains the following items in a frame per method:

- The local variable area

- Saved context of the caller

- The operand stack

A possible implementation of this layout is shown in Figure 5.10. A method with two arguments, arg_1 and arg_2 (arg_0 is the *this* pointer), is invoked in this example. The invoked method *sees* the arguments as var_1 and var_2. var_3 is the only local variable of the method. SP is a pointer to the top of stack and VP points to the start of the variable area.

5.5.2 Access Patterns on the Java Stack

The pipelined architecture of a Java processor executes basic instructions in a single cycle. A stack that contains the operand stack *and* the local variables results in following access patterns:

Stack Operation: Read of the two top elements, operate on them and push back the result on the top of the stack. The pipeline stages for this operation are:

```
value1 ← stack[sp], value2 ← stack[sp-1]
result ← value1 op value2, sp ← sp-1
stack[sp] ← result
```

Variable Load: Read of a data element deeper down in the stack, relative to a variable base address pointer (VP), and push this data on the top of the stack. This operation needs two pipeline stages:

```
value ← stack[vp+offset], sp ← sp+1
stack[sp] ← value
```

Variable Store: Pop the top element of the stack and write it in the variable relative to the variable base address:

```
value ← stack[sp]
stack[vp+offset] ← value, sp ← sp-1
```

For pipelined execution of these operations, a three-port memory or register file (two read ports and one write port) is necessary.

5.5.3 Common Realizations of a Stack Cache

As the stack is a heavily accessed memory region, the stack – or part of it – has to be placed in the upper level of the memory hierarchy. This part of the stack is referred to as *stack cache* in this thesis. As described in [40], a typical memory hierarchy contains the following elements, with increasing access time and size:

- CPU register

- On-chip cache memory

- Off-chip cache memory

- Main memory

- Magnetic disk for virtual memory

For a stack cache, a register file is the solution with the shortest access time. However, in order to store more than a few elements in the cache, an on-chip memory realization can provide a larger cache. Both variants have been used and are described below.

The Register File as a Stack Cache

An example of a Java processor that uses a register file is Sun's picoJava [89]. It contains 64 registers, organized as a circular buffer. To compensate for this *small* stack cache, an automatic spill and fill circuit needs another read/write port to the register file. aJile's JEMCore [37] is a direct-execution Java processor core that contains 24 registers. Only six of them are used to cache the top elements of the stack. With this small register count, local variables are not part of the cache. The Ignite [77] (formerly known as PSC1000) is a stack processor, originally designed as a Forth processor and now promoted as a Java processor, has an operand stack that contains 18 registers with automatic spill and fill.

A basic pipeline for a stack processor with a register file contains the following stages:

1. IF – instruction fetch

2. ID – instruction decode

3. EX – read register file and execute

4. WB – write result back to register file

With this pipeline structure, a single data-forwarding path between WB and EX is necessary. The ALU with the register file (with a size of 16, a common size for RISC processors) and the bypass unit are shown in Figure 5.11. In Table 5.8 the hardware resources of this type of stack cache are approximated, using the values given in Table 5.7 (a MUX not found in this table is assumed to use combinations of the basic types; e.g. two 8:1 and one 2:1 for a 16:1). An experimental evaluation of this architecture in an FPGA is described in Section 5.5.5.

Basic function	Gate count
D-Flip-Flop	5
2:1 MUX	3
4:1 MUX	5
8:1 MUX	9
SRAM Bit	1.5

Table 5.7: Simplified gate count for basic functions

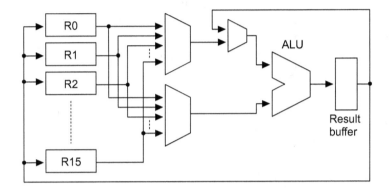

Figure 5.11: A stack cache with registers

Function block	Basic function	Gate count
Register File	512 D-Flip-Flops	2,560
Read MUX	2x32 16:1 MUX	1,344
Forward MUX	32 2:1 MUX	96
ALU buffer	32 D-Flip-Flops	160
Total		4,160

Table 5.8: Estimated gate count for a register stack cache

On-chip Memory as a Stack Cache

Using SRAM on the chip provides a *large* stack cache (e.g. 128 entries). However, as we have seen in Section 5.5.2, a three-port memory is necessary. An additional pipeline stage performs the cache memory read:

1. IF – instruction fetch

2. ID – instruction decode

3. RD – memory read

4. EX – execute

5. WB – write result back to memory

With this pipeline structure, two data forwarding paths are necessary. The resulting architecture is shown in Figure 5.12 and a gate count estimate is provided in Table 5.9. This version needs 70% more resources than the first one, but provides an eight times larger stack cache.

Example designs that use this kind of stack cache are (i) Komodo [95], a Java processor intended as a basis for research on multithreaded real-time scheduling, and (ii) FemtoJava [45], a research project to build an application specific Java processor.

A three-port memory is an expensive option for an ASIC and unusual in an FPGA. It can be emulated in an FPGA by two memories with a single read and write port. The write data is written in both memory blocks and each memory block provides a different read port. However, this solution also doubles the amount of memory.

Both designs (Komodo and FemtoJava) avoid the memory doubling by serializing the two reads. This serialization results in minimum of two clock cycles execution time for basic instructions or halves the clock frequency of the whole pipeline.

5.5.4 A Two-Level Stack Cache

In this section, we will discuss access patterns of the JVM and their implication on the functional units of the pipeline. A faster and smaller architecture is proposed for the stack cache of a Java processor.

JVM Stack Access Revised

If we analyze the JVM's access patterns to the stack in more detail, we can see that a two-port read is only performed with the two top elements of the stack. All other operations with elements deeper in the stack, local variables load and store, only need

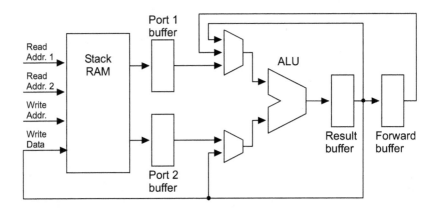

Figure 5.12: A stack cache with on-chip RAM

Function block	Basic function	Gate count
Stack RAM	e.g. 128x32 Bits	6, 144
Port buffer	2x32 D-Flip-Flops	320
Forward MUX	32x 2:1 MUX, 3:1 MUX	288
ALU buffer	2x32 D-Flip-Flops	320
Total		7, 072

Table 5.9: Estimated gate count for a stack cache with RAM

one read port. If we only implement the two top elements of the stack in registers, we can use a standard on-chip RAM with one read and one write port.

We will show that all operations can be performed with this configuration. Let A be the top-of-stack, B the element below top-of-stack. The memory that serves as the second level cache is represented by the array sm. Two indices in this array are used: p points to the logical third element of the stack and changes as the stack grows or shrinks, v points to the base of the local variables area in the stack and n is the address offset of a variable. op is a two operand stack operation with a single result (i.e. a typical ALU operation).

Case 1: ALU operation

$A \leftarrow A\ op\ B$
$B \leftarrow sm[p]$
$p \leftarrow p - 1$

The two operands are provided by the two top level registers. A single read access from sm is necessary to fill B with a new value.

Case 2: Variable load (*Push*)

$sm[p+1] \leftarrow B$
$B \leftarrow A$
$A \leftarrow sm[v+n]$
$p \leftarrow p + 1$

One read access from sm is necessary for the variable read. The former TOS value moves down to B and the data previously in B is written to sm.

Case 3: Variable store (*Pop*)

$sm[v+n] \leftarrow A$
$A \leftarrow B$
$B \leftarrow sm[p]$
$p \leftarrow p - 1$

The TOS value is written to sm. A is filled with B and B is filled in an identical manner to Case 1, needing a single read access from sm.

We can see that all three basic operations can be performed with a stack memory with one read and one write port. Assuming a memory is used that can handle concurrent read and write access, there is no structural access conflict between A, B and sm. That means that all operations can be performed concurrently in a single cycle.

As we can see in Figure 5.10 the operand stack and the local variables area are distinct regions of the stack. A concurrent read from and write to the stack is only performed on a variable load or store. When the read is from the local variables area the write goes to the operand area; a read from the operand area is concurrent with a write to the local variables area. Therefore there is no concurrent read and write to the same location in *sm*. There is no constraint on the read-during-write behavior of the memory (old data, undefined or new data), which simplifies the memory design. In a design where read and write-back are located in different pipeline stages, as in the architectures described above, either the memory must provide the new data on a read-during-write, or external forward logic is necessary.

From the three cases described, we can derive the memory addresses for the read and write port of the memory, as shown in Table 5.10.

Read address	Write address
p	p+1
v+n	v+n

Table 5.10: Stack memory addresses

The Datapath

The architecture of the two-level stack cache can be seen in Figure 5.13. Register A represents the top-of-stack and register B the data below the top-of-stack. ALU operations are performed with these two registers and the result is placed in A. During such an ALU operation, B is filled with new data from the stack RAM. A new value from the local variable area is loaded directly from the stack RAM into A. The data previously in A is moved to B and the data from B is spilled to the stack RAM. A is stored in the stack RAM on a store instruction to the local variable. The data from B is moved to A and B is filled with a new value from the stack RAM.

With this architecture, the pipeline can be reduced to three stages:

1. IF – instruction fetch

2. ID – instruction decode

3. EX – execute, load or store

The estimated resource usage of this two-level stack cache architecture is given in Table 5.11. It can be seen that this architecture is roughly as complex as the solution given above (about 5% less gates). However, the reduced complexity with the two-port RAM instead of a three-port RAM is not included in the table. The critical path through the ALU contains only one 2:1 MUX to register A in this solution, rather than one 3:1 MUX in one ALU path and one 2:1 MUX in the other ALU path. As no data forwarding logic is necessary, the decoding logic is also simpler.

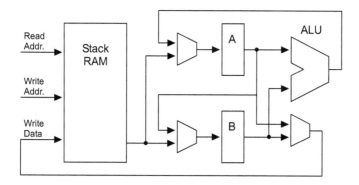

Figure 5.13: Two-level stack cache

Function block	Basic function	Gate count
Stack RAM	e. g. 128x32 Bits	6,144
TOS, TOS-1 buffer	2x32 D-Flip-Flops	320
Three MUX	3x32 2:1 MUX	288
Total		6,752

Table 5.11: Estimated gate count for a two-level stack cache

Data Forwarding – A Non-Issue

Data dependencies in the instruction stream result in the so-called *data hazards* [40] in the pipeline. Data forwarding is a technique that moves data from a later pipeline stage back to an earlier one to solve this problem. The term *forward* is correct in the temporal domain as data is transferred to an instruction in the future. However, it is misleading in the structural domain as the forward direction is towards the *last* pipeline stage for an instruction.

As the probability of data dependency is very high in a stack-based architecture, one would expect several data forwarding paths to be necessary. However, in the two-level architecture proposed, with its resulting three-stage pipeline, no data hazards will occur and no data forwarding is therefore necessary. This simplifies the decoding stage and reduces the number of multiplexers in the execution path. We will show that none of the three data hazard types [40] are an issue in this architecture. With instructions i and j, where i is issued before j, the data hazard types are:

Read after write: j reads a source before i writes it. This is the most common type of hazard and, in the architectures described above, is solved by using the ALU buffers and the forwarding multiplexer in the ALU datapath. On a stack architecture, write takes three forms:

- Implicit write of TOS during an ALU operation

- Write to the TOS during a load instruction

- Write to an arbitrary entry of the stack with a store instruction

A read also occurs in three different forms:

- Read two top values from the stack for an ALU operation

- Read TOS for a store instruction

- Read an arbitrary entry of the stack with the load instruction

With the two top elements of the stack as discrete registers, these values are read, operated on and written back in the same cycle. No read that depends on TOS or TOS-1 suffers from a data hazard. Read and write access to a local variable is also performed in the same pipeline stage. Thus, the read after write order is not affected. However, there is also an additional hidden read and write - the fill and spill of register B:

- *B fill:* *B* is written during an ALU operation and on a variable store. During an ALU operation, the operands are the values from *A* and the old value from *B*. The new value for *B* is read from the stack memory and does not depend on the new value of *A*. During a variable store operation, *A* is written to the stack memory and does not depend on *B*. The new value for *B* is also read from the stack memory and it is not obvious that this value does not depend on the written value. However, the variable area and the operand stack are distinct areas in the stack (this changes only on method invocation and return), guaranteeing that concurrent read/write access does not produce a data hazard.

- *B spill:* *B* is read on a load operation. The new value of *B* is the old value of *A* and does not therefore depend on the stack memory read. *B* is written to the stack. For the read value from the stack memory that goes to *A*, the argument concerning the distinct stack areas in the case of *B fill* described above still applies.

Write after read: *j* writes a destination before it is read by *i*. This cannot take place as all reads and writes are performed in the same pipeline stage keeping the instruction order.

Write after write: *j* writes an operand before it is written by *i*. This hazard is not present in this architecture as all writes are performed in the same pipeline stage.

5.5.5 Resource Usage Compared

The three architectures described above are implemented in Altera's EP1C6Q240C6 [16] FPGA. The three-port memory for the second solution is emulated with two embedded memory blocks. The ALU for this comparison is kept simple with the following functions: NOP, ADD, SUB, POP, AND, OR, XOR and load external data. The load of external data is necessary in order to prevent the synthesizer from optimizing away the whole design. A real implementation of an ALU for a Java processor, as described in Section 5.4, is a little bit more complex with a barrel shifter and additional load paths. In order to gain the maximum operating frequency for the design, the testbed for this architecture contains registers for the external data, the RAM address buses, and the control and select signals. Table 5.12 shows the resource usage and maximum operation frequency of the three different architectures.

LC stands for 'Logic Cell' and is the basic element in an FPGA: a 4-bit lookup table with a register. The LC count in the table includes the register count. The ALU alone without any stack cache needs 194 LCs. In the first line, the testbed is

Design	Total		Cache		Memory	fmax	Size
	LCs	Reg.	LCs	Reg.	[bit]	[MHz]	[word]
Testbed w. ALU	261	166	-	-	-	237	-
16 register cache	968	657	707	491	0	110	16
SRAM cache	372	185	111	19	8,192	153	128
Two-level cache	373	184	112	18	4,096	213	130

Table 5.12: Resource and performance compared

combined with the ALU without any stack caching, as a reference design. With this configuration, we can obtain the maximum possible speed of the registered ALU in this FPGA technology, in this case an operating frequency of 237MHz or a 4.2 ns delay. This value is an upper bound of the system frequency. Every pipelined architecture needs one or more multiplexer in the ALU path, either for data forwarding or for operand selection, resulting in a longer delay. The fourth and fifth columns represent the resource usage of the cache logic without the testbed and ALU. The last column shows the effective cache size in data words.

The version with the 16 registers was synthesized with two different synthesizer settings. In the first setting, the register file is implemented with discrete registers while, with a different setting, the register file is automatically implemented in two 32-bits embedded RAM blocks. Two different RAM blocks are necessary to provide two read ports and one write port. In both versions, the delay time to read the register file (delay through the 16:1 MUX of 4.9 ns or RAM access time of 4.6 ns) is in the same order as the delay time through the ALU, resulting in a system frequency of half the theoretical frequency of that with the ALU alone. As the structure of the version with the embedded RAM block is very similar with the SRAM cache, only the version with the discrete registers is shown in Table 5.12.

The stack cache with a RAM and registers on the RAM output (the additional pipeline stage) performs better than the first solution. However, the 3:1 MUX in the critical path still adds 2.3 ns to the delay time. Compared with the proposed solution (in the last line), we see that double the amount of RAM is needed for the two read ports.

The two-level stack cache solution performs at 213MHz, i.e. almost the theoretical system frequency (in practice, about 10% slower). Only a 2:1 MUX is added to the critical path. The single read port memory needs half the number of memory bits of the other two solutions.

5.5.6 Summary

In this section, the stack architecture of the JVM was analyzed. We have seen that the JVM is different from the classical stack architecture. The JVM uses the stack both as an operand stack *and* as the storage place for local variables. Local variables are placed in the stack at a *deeper* position. To load and store these variables, an access path to an arbitrary position in the stack is necessary. As the stack is the most frequently accessed memory area in the JVM, caching of this memory is mandatory for a high-performing Java processor.

A common solution, found in a number of different Java processors, is to implement this stack cache as a standard three-port register file with additional support to address this register file in a stack like manner. The architectures presented above differ in the realization of the register file: as a discrete register or in on-chip memory. Implementing the stack cache as discrete registers is very expensive. A three-port memory is also an expensive option for an ASIC and unusual in an FPGA. It can be emulated by two memories with a single read and write port. However, this solution also doubles the amount of memory.

Detailed analysis of the access patterns to the stack showed that only the two top elements of the stack are accessed in a single cycle. Given this fact, the proposed architecture uses registers to cache only the two top elements of the stack. The next level of the stack cache is provided by a simple on-chip memory. The memory automatically spills and fills the second register. Implementing the two top elements of the stack as fixed registers, instead of elements that are indexed by a stack pointer, also greatly simplifies the overall pipeline.

The proposed stack architecture has the following advantages: (i) Simpler cache memory results in having half the memory usage of the other solutions in an FPGA. (ii) Minimal impact on the raw speed of the ALU. Operates at almost the theoretical maximum system frequency of the ALU. (iii) Single read, execute and write-back pipeline stage results in an overall 3-stage pipeline processor design. (iv) No data forwarding is necessary, which simplifies instruction decode logic and reduces the multiplexer count in the critical path.

5.6 HW/SW Codesign

Using a hardware description language and loading the design in an FPGA the former strict border between hardware and software gets blurred. Is configuring an FPGA not more like loading a program for execution?

This looser distinction makes it possible to move functions easily between hardware and software resulting in a highly configurable design. If speed is an issue, more functions are realized in hardware. If cost is the primary concern these functions are moved to software and a smaller FPGA can be used. Let us examine these possibilities on a relatively expensive function: multiplication.

In Java bytecode imul performs a 32 bit signed multiplication with a 32 bit result. There are no exceptions on overflow. Since 32 bit single cycle multiplications are far beyond the possibilities of current, mainstream FPGAs the first solution is a sequential multiplier.

Sequential Booth Multiplier in VHDL   Listing 5.5 shows the VHDL code of the multiplier. Two microcode instructions are used to access this function: stmul stores the two operands (from TOS and TOS-1) and starts the sequential multiplier. After 33 cycles, the result is loaded with ldmul. Listing 5.6 shows the microcode for imul.

Multiplication in Microcode   If we run out of resources in the FPGA, we can move the function to microcode. The implementation of imul is almost identical with the Java code in Listing 5.7 and needs 73 microcode instructions.

Bytecode imul in Java   Microcode is stored in an embedded memory block of the FPGA. This is also a resource of the FPGA. We can move the code to external memory by implementing imul in Java bytecode. Bytecodes not implemented in microcode result in a static Java method call from a special class (com.jopdesign.sys.JVM). This class has prototypes for each bytecode ordered by the bytecode value. This allows us to find the right method by indexing the method table with the value of the bytecode. Listing 5.7 shows the Java method for imul. The additional overhead for this implementation is a call and return with cache refills.

Implementations Compared   Table 5.13 lists the resource usage and execution time for the three implementations. Execution time is measured with both operands negative, the worst-case execution time for the software implementations. The implementation in Java is slower than the microcode implementation as the Java method is loaded from main memory into the bytecode cache.

Only a few lines of code have to be changed to select one of the three implementations. The shown principle can also be applied to other expensive bytecodes: e.g. idiv, ishr, iushr and ishl. As a result, the resource usage of JOP is highly configurable and can be selected for each application according to the needs of the application. Treating VHDL as a software language allows easy movement of function blocks between hardware and software.

```
process(clk, wr_a, wr_b)

    variable count  : integer range 0 to width;
    variable pa     : signed(64) downto 0);
    variable a_1    : std_logic;
    alias p         : signed(32 downto 0)
                      is pa(64 downto 32);

begin
    if rising_edge(clk) then
        if wr_a='1' then
            p := (others => '0');
            pa(width-1 downto 0) := signed(din);

        elsif wr_b='1' then
            b <= din;
            a_1 := '0';
            count := width;
        else
            if count > 0 then
                case std_ulogic_vector'(pa(0), a_1) is
                    when "01" =>
                        p := p + signed(b);
                    when "10" =>
                        p := p - signed(b);
                    when others =>
                        null;
                end case;
                a_1 := pa(0);
                pa := shift_right(pa, 1);
                count := count - 1;
            end if;
        end if;
    end if;
    dout <= std_logic_vector(pa(31 downto 0));
end process;
```

Listing 5.5: Booth multiplier in VHDL

```
imul:
            stmul           // store both operands and start
            pop             // pop second operand

            ldi 5           // 6*5+3 cycles wait
imul_loop:                  // wait loop
            dup
            nop
            bnz imul_loop
            ldi -1          // decrement in branch slot
            add

            pop             // remove counter

            ldmul   nxt // load result
```

Listing 5.6: Microcode to access the Booth multiplier

	Hardware [LC]	Microcode [Byte]	Time [Cycle]
VHDL	156	10	35
Microcode	0	73	750
Java	0	0	2,300

Table 5.13: Different implementations of imul compared

```
public static int imul(int a, int b) {

    int c, i;
    boolean neg = false;
    if (a<0) {
        neg = true;
        a = -a;
    }
    if (b<0) {
        neg = !neg;
        b = -b;
    }
    c = 0;
    for (i=0; i<32; ++i) {
        c <<= 1;
        if ((a & 0x80000000)!=0) c += b;
        a <<= 1;
    }
    if (neg) c = -c;
    return c;
}
```

Listing 5.7: Implementation of bytecode imul in Java

5.7 Real-Time Predictability

General-purpose processors are optimized for average throughput and non real-time operating systems are responsible for fair and efficient scheduling of resources. Real-time systems need a processor with low and known WCET of instructions. Real-time operating systems have properties, such as fast interrupt response, rapid context switch, short blocking times and a scheduler that implements a simple, in most cases strict priority driven, scheduling algorithm. This section describes design decisions for JOP to support such real-time systems.

5.7.1 Interrupts

Interrupts are usually associated with low-level programming of device drivers. The priorities of interrupts and their handler functions are above task priorities and yield to an immediate context switch. In this form, interrupts cannot be integrated in a schedule with *normal* tasks. The execution time of the interrupt handler has to be integrated in the schedulability analysis as additional blocking time. A better solution is to handle interrupts, which represent external events, as schedulable objects with priority levels in the range of real-time tasks, as suggested in the RTSJ.

The Timer Interrupt   The timer or clock interrupt has a different semantic than other interrupts. The main purpose of the timer interrupt is representation of time and release of periodic or time triggered tasks. One common implementation is a clock tick. The interrupt occurs at a regular interval (e.g. 10 ms) and a decision has to be taken whether a task has to be released. This approach is simple to implement, but there are two major drawbacks: The resolution of timed events is bound by the resolution of the clock tick and clock ticks without a task switch are a waste of execution time.

A better approach, used in JOP, is to generate timer interrupts at the release times of the tasks. The scheduler is now responsible for reprogramming the timer after each occurrence of a timer interrupt. The list of sleeping threads has to be searched to find the nearest release time in the future of a higher priority thread than the one that will be released now. This time is used for the next timer interrupt.

External Events   Hardware interrupts, other than the timer interrupt, are represented as asynchronous events with an associated thread. This means that the event is a *normal* schedulable object under the control of the scheduler. With a minimum interarrival time, enforced by hardware, these events can be incorporated into the priority assignment and schedulability analysis in the same way as periodic tasks.

Software Interrupts   The common software generated interrupts, such as illegal memory access or divide by zero, are represented by Java runtime exceptions and need no special handler. They can be detected with a try-catch block.

Asynchronous notification from the program is supported, in the same way as an external event, as a schedulable object with an associated thread. The event is triggered through the call of fire(). The thread with the handler is placed in the runnable state and scheduled according to priority.

Hardware Failures   Serious hardware failures, such as illegal opcode or parity error from the memory systems, lead to a shutdown of the system. However, a *last try* to call a handler that changes the state of the system to a safe state and inform an upper level system, can improve the integrity of the overall system.

5.7.2 Task Switch

An important issue in real-time systems is the time for a task switch. A task switch consists of two actions:

- *Scheduling* is the selection of the task order and timing

- *Dispatching* is the term for the context switch between tasks

Scheduling   Most real-time systems use a fixed-priority preemptive scheduler. Tasks with the same priority are usually scheduled in a FIFO order. Two common ways to assign priorities are rate monotonic or, in a more general form, deadline monotonic assignment. When two tasks get the same priority, we can choose one of them and assign a higher priority to that task and the task set is still schedulable. We get a strictly monotonic priority order and do not have to deal with FIFO order. This eliminates queues for each priority level and results in a single, priority ordered task list.

Strictly fixed priority schedulers suffer from a problem called *priority inversion* [84]. The problem where a low priority task blocks a high priority task on a shared resource is solved by raising the priority of the low priority task. Two standard priority inversion avoidance protocols are common:

Priority Inheritance Protocol: A lock assigns the priority of the highest-priority waiting task to the task holding the lock until that task releases the resource.

Priority Ceiling Emulation Protocol: A lock gets a priority assigned above the priority of the highest-priority task that will ever acquire the lock. Every task will be immediately assigned the priority of that lock when acquiring it.

The priority inheritance protocol is more complex to implement and the time when the priority of a task is raised is not so obvious. It is not raised because the task does anything, but because another task reaches some point in its execution path.

Using priority ceiling emulation with unique priorities, different from task priorities, the priority order is still strictly monotonic. The priority ordered task list is expanded with slots for each lock. If a task acquires a lock, it is placed in the corresponding slot. With this extension to the task list, scheduling is still simple and can be efficiently implemented.

Dispatching   The time for a context switch depends on the size of the state of the tasks. For a stack machine it is not so obvious what belongs to the state of a task. If the stack resides in main memory, only a few registers (e.g. program counter and stack pointer) need to be saved and restored. However, the stack is a frequently accessed memory region of the JVM. The stack can be seen as a data cache and should be placed near the execution unit (in this case, *near* means on the chip and not in external memory). However, on-chip memory is usually too small to hold the stack content for all tasks. This means that the stack is part of the execution context and has to be saved and restored on a context switch.

In JOP, the stack is placed in local (on-chip) FPGA memory with single cycle access time. With this configuration, the next question is how much of the stack to place there. Either the complete stack of a thread or only the stack frame of the current method can reside locally. If the complete stack of a thread is stored in local memory, the invocation of methods and returns are fast, but the context is large. For fast context switches, it is preferable to have only a short stack in local memory. This results in less data being transferred to and from main memory, but more memory transfers on method invocation and return. The local stack can be further divided into small pieces, each holding only one stack frame of one thread. During the context switch, only the stack pointer needs to be saved and restored. The outcome of this is a very fast context switch, although the size of the local memory limits the maximum number of threads.

Since JOP is a soft-core processor, these different solutions can be configured for different application requirements. It is even possible to mix of these policies: some stack slots can be assigned to *important* threads, while the remaining threads share one slot. This stack slot only needs to be exchanged with the main memory when switching *to* a less *important* thread.

5.7.3 Architectural Design Decisions

In hard real-time systems, meeting temporal requirements is of the same importance as functional correctness. This results in different architectural constraints than in a design for a non real-time system. A low upper bound of the execution time is of premium importance. Good average execution time is useless for a pure hard real-time system.

Common architectural components, found in general purpose processors to enhance average performance, are usually problematic for the WCET analysis. A pragmatic approach to this problem is to ignore these features for the analysis. With a processor designed for real-time applications, these features have to be substituted by predictable architecture enhancements.

Branch Prediction As the pipelines of current general-purpose processors get longer to support higher clock rates the penalty of branches get too high. This is compensated by branch prediction logic with branch target buffers. However, the upper bound of the branch execution time is the same as without this feature. In JOP, branch prediction is avoided. This results in pressure on the pipeline length. The core processor has a pipeline length of as little as three stages resulting in a branch execution time of three cycles in microcode. The two slots in the branch delay can be filled with instructions or *nop*. With the additional bytecode fetch and translation stage, the overall pipeline is four stages and results in a four cycle execution time for a bytecode branch.

Caches and Instruction Prefetch To reduce the growing gap between the clock frequency of the processor and memory access times multi-level cache architectures are commonly used. Since even a single level cache is problematic for WCET analysis, more levels in the memory architecture are almost not analyzable. The additional levels also increase the latency of memory access on a cache miss.

In a stack machine, the stack is a frequently accessed memory area. This makes the stack an ideal candidate to be placed near the execution unit in the memory hierarchy. In JOP the stack is implemented as internal memory with the two top elements as explicit registers. This single cycle memory can be seen as a data cache. However, unlike in picoJava, this limited memory is not automatically spilled and filled. Automatically spill and fill introduces unpredictable access to the main memory. Data exchange between internal stack and main memory is under program control and can be done on method invocation/return or on a thread switch.

The next most accessed memory area is the code area. A simple prefetch queue, as it is found in older processors, could increase instruction throughput after executing a multi-cycle bytecode. For a stream of single cycle bytecodes, prefetching is useless and the frequent occurrence of branches and method invocations, about 12–23% (see Section 5.1) in typical Java programs, reduces the performance gain. The prefetch queue also results in (probably unbounded) execution time dependencies over a stream of instructions, which complicates timing analysis.

JOP has a method cache with a novel replace policy. Since typical methods in Java programs are short and there are only relative branches in a method, a complete method is loaded in the cache on invocation and on return. This cache fill strategy lumps all cache misses together and is very simple to analyze. It also simplifies the hardware of the cache since no tag memory or address translation is necessary. The *romizer* tool JavaCodeCompact checks the maximum allowed method size. Section 5.8 describes the proposed cache solution in detail. Memory areas for the heap and class description with the constant pool are not cached in JOP.

Superscalar Processors   A superscalar processor consists of several execution units and tries to extract instruction level parallelism (ILP) with out of order execution. Again, this is a nightmare for timing analysis. The code for a stack machine has less implicit parallelism than a register machine.

One form of enhancement, usually implemented in stack machines, is instruction folding. The instruction stream is scanned to find frequent patterns like load-load-add-store and substitutes these four instructions with one, RISC-like, operation. There are two issues with instruction folding in JOP: The combined instruction needs two read and one write access to the stack in a single cycle. This would result in doubling of the internal memory usage in the FPGA. It also needs, at minimum, four bytes read access to the method cache. To overcome word boundaries, prefetching has to be introduced after the method cache. This results in an additional pipeline stage, time dependency of instructions with a more complex analysis and more hardware resources for the multiplexers.

Programs for embedded and real-time systems are usually multi-threaded. In future work, it will be investigated if the additional hardware resources needed for ILP can be better used with additional processor cores utilizing this implicit thread-level parallelism.

Garbage Collection   As use of the heap is avoided in hard real-time systems, no garbage collector is implemented. Without a garbage collector, the memory layout of objects can be simplified. Every reference points directly to the object. No indirection through a handle, which would simplify memory compaction in the garbage collector, is needed. This reduces access time to object fields and methods.

Time-Predictable Instructions   A good model of a processor with accurate timing information is essential for a tight WCET analysis. The architecture of JOP and the microcode are designed with this in mind. Execution time of bytecodes is known cycle accurately (see Section 7.4 and Appendix D). It is possible to analyze the WCET on the bytecode level [7] without the uncertainties of an interpreting JVM [5] or generated native code from ahead-of-time compilers for Java.

5.7.4 Summary

In this section, we argued that, while common techniques in processor architectures increase average throughput, they are not feasible for real-time systems. The influence of these architectural enhancements is at best hardly WCET-analyzable.

The proposed alternatives influence the processor architecture, as described in earlier sections, as well as the software architecture that will be described in Section 6.1.

However, the most important architectural enhancement for pipelined machines is caching, which is necessary even in embedded systems. We have shown in Section 5.5 how a time-predictable data cache for a stack machine can be implemented. In the following section, we will propose a time-predictable cache for instructions.

5.8 A Time-Predictable Instruction Cache

Worst-case execution time (WCET) analysis [78] of real-time programs is essential for any schedulability analysis. To provide a low WCET value, a good processor model is necessary. However, the architectural advancement in modern processor designs is dominated by the rule: *'Make the common case fast'*. This is the opposite of *'Reduce the worst case'* and complicates WCET analysis.

Cache memory for the instructions and data is a classic example of this paradigm. Avoiding or ignoring this feature in real-time systems, due to its unpredictable behavior, results in a very pessimistic WCET value. Plenty of effort has gone into research into integrating the instruction cache in the timing analysis of tasks [4, 38, 58] and the influence of the cache on task preemption [57, 11]. The influence of different cache architectures on WCET analysis is described in [39].

We will tackle this problem from the architectural side – an instruction cache organization in which simpler and more accurate WCET analysis is more important than average case performance.

In this section, we will propose a method cache with a novel replacement policy. In Java bytecode only relative branches exist, and a method is therefore only left when a return instruction has been executed[6]. It has been observed that methods are typically short (see Section 5.1.2) in Java applications. These properties are utilized by a cache architecture that stores complete methods. A complete method is loaded into the cache on both invocation and return. This cache fill strategy lumps all cache misses together and is very simple to analyze.

5.8.1 Cache Performance

In real-time systems we prefer time-predictable architectures over those with a high average performance. However, performance is still important. In this section, we will give a short overview of the formulas from [40] that are used to calculate the cache's influence on execution time. We will extend the single measurement *miss rate* to a two value set, memory read and transaction rate, that is architecture independent and better reflects the two properties (bandwidth and latency) of the main memory. To evaluate cache performance, MEM_{clk} memory stall cycles are added to the CPU execution time (t_{exe}) equation:

$$t_{exe} = (CPU_{clk} + MEM_{clk}) \times t_{clk}$$
$$MEM_{clk} = Misses \times MP_{clk}$$

The miss penalty MP_{clk} is the cost per miss, measured in clock cycles. When the instruction count IC is given as the number of instructions executed, CPI the average clock cycles per instruction and the number of misses per instruction, we obtain the following result:

$$CPU_{clk} = IC \times CPI_{exe}$$
$$MEM_{clk} = IC \times \frac{Misses}{Instruction} \times MP_{clk}$$
$$t_{exe} = IC \times (CPI_{exe} + \frac{Misses}{Instruction} \times MP_{clk}) \times t_{clk}$$

As this section is only concerned with the instruction cache, we will split the memory stall cycles into misses caused by the instruction fetch and misses caused by data access.

$$CPI = CPI_{exe} + CPI_{IM} + CPI_{DM}$$

CPI_{exe} is the average number of clock cycles per instruction, given an ideal memory system without any stalls. CPI_{IM} are the additional clock cycles caused by instruction cache misses and CPI_{DM} the data miss portion of the CPI. This split between

---

[6]An uncaught exception also results in a method exit.

instruction and data portions of the CPI better reflects the split of the cache between instruction and data cache found in actual processors. The misses per instruction are often given as misses per 1000 instructions. However, there are several drawbacks to using a single number:

Architecture dependent: The average number of memory accesses per instruction differs greatly between a RISC processor and the Java Virtual Machine (JVM). A typical RISC processor needs one memory word (4 bytes) per instruction word, and about 40% of the instructions [40] are *load* or *store* instructions. Using the example of a 32-bit RISC processor, this results in 5.6 bytes memory access per instruction. The average length of a JVM bytecode instruction is 1.7 bytes and about 18% of the instructions access the memory for data load and store.

Block size dependent: Misses per instruction depends subtly on the block size. On a single cache miss, a whole block of the cache is filled. Therefore, the probability that a future instruction request is a hit is higher with a larger block size. However, a larger block size results in a higher miss penalty as more memory is transferred.

Main memory is usually composed of DRAMs. Access time to this memory is measured in terms of latency (the time taken to access the first word of a larger block) and bandwidth (the number of bytes read or written in a single request per time unit). These two values, along with the block size of a cache, are used to calculate the miss penalty:

$$MP_{clk} = Latency + \frac{Block\ size}{Bandwidth}$$

To better evaluate different cache organizations and different instruction sets (RISC versus JVM), we will introduce two performance measurements – memory bytes read per instruction byte and memory transactions per instruction byte:

$$MBIB = \frac{Memory\ bytes\ read}{Instruction\ bytes}$$

$$MTIB = \frac{Memory\ transactions}{Instruction\ bytes}$$

These two measures are closely related to memory bandwidth and latency. With these two values and the properties of the main memory, we can calculate the average memory cycles per instruction byte $MCIB$ and CPI_{IM}, i.e. the values we are concerned in this section.

$$MCIB = (\frac{MBIB}{Bandwith} + MTIB \times Latency)$$
$$CPI_{IM} = MCIB \times Instruction\ length$$

The misses per instruction can be converted to MBIB and MTIB when the following parameters are known: the average instruction length of the architecture, the block size of the cache and the miss penalty in latency and bandwidth. We will examine this further in the following example:

We use the following architecture to illustrate the conversion: a RISC architecture with a 4 bytes instruction length, an 8KB instruction cache with 64-byte blocks and a miss rate of 8.16 per 1000 instructions [40]. The miss penalty is 100 clock cycles. The memory system is assumed to deliver one word (4 bytes) per cycle.

Firstly, we need to calculate the latency of the memory system.

$$Latency = MP_{clk} - \frac{Blocksize}{Bandwidth}$$
$$= 100 - \frac{64}{4} = 84\ \text{clock cycles}$$

With $Miss\ rate = \frac{Cache\ miss}{Cache\ access}$, we obtain MBIB.

$$MBIB = \frac{Memory\ bytes\ read}{Instruction\ bytes}$$
$$= \frac{Cache\ miss \times Block\ size}{Cache\ access \times Instruction\ length}$$
$$= Miss\ rate \times \frac{Block\ size}{Instruction\ length}$$
$$= 8.16 \times 10^{-3} \times \frac{65}{4}$$
$$= 0.131$$

MTIB is calculated in a similar way:

$$
\begin{aligned}
MTIB &= \frac{Memory\ transactions}{Instruction\ bytes} \\
&= \frac{Cache\ miss}{Cache\ access \times Instruction\ length} \\
&= \frac{Miss\ rate}{Instruction\ length} \\
&= \frac{8.16 \times 10^{-3}}{4} \\
&= 2.04 \times 10^{-3}
\end{aligned}
$$

For a quick check, we can calculate CPI_{IM}:

$$
\begin{aligned}
MCIB &= \frac{MBIB}{Bandwith} + MTIB \times Latency \\
&= \frac{0.131}{4} + 2.04 \times 10^{-3} \times 84 \\
&= 0.204 \\
CPI_{IM} &= MCIB \times Instruction\ length \\
&= 0.204 \times 4 \\
&= 0.816
\end{aligned}
$$

This is the same value as that which we get from using the miss rate with the miss penalty:

$$
\begin{aligned}
CPI_{IM} &= Miss\ rate \times Miss\ penalty \\
&= 8.16 \times 10^{-3} \times 100 \\
&= 0.816
\end{aligned}
$$

However, MBIB and MTIB are architecture independent and better reflect the latency and bandwidth of the main memory.

5.8.2 Proposed Cache Solution

In this section, we will develop a solution for a predictable cache. Typical Java programs consist of short methods. There are no branches out of the method and all branches inside are relative. In the proposed architecture, the full code of a method is loaded into the cache before execution. The cache is filled on invocations and returns. This means that all cache fills are lumped together with a known execution time. The full loaded method and relative addressing inside a method also result in a simpler cache. Tag memory and address translation are not necessary.

However, we will first discuss an even simpler solution – no caching at all. Without an instruction cache, prefetching is mandatory, especially with a variable length instruction set. The issues surrounding prefetching are discussed in the next section.

Instruction Prefetching

A simple prefetch queue, as found in older processors, can increase instruction throughput after a multi-cycle bytecode is executed. However, for a stream of single-cycle bytecodes, prefetching is useless and the frequent occurrence of branches, method invocations, and method returns (see Section 5.1) reduces the performance gain. Using a prefetch queue also results in execution time dependencies over a stream of instructions, which complicates timing analysis.

For a variable length instruction set, prefetching is also not a straightforward option. The prefetching unit needs to guarantee the availability of a complete instruction for the fetch unit. As the actual length of the instruction is not known at this stage, the prefetch unit must be a minimum of $maximum\ length - 1$ bytes ahead of the requested instruction. This can lead to unnecessary memory transfers. The return instruction is a typical example of this. It is 1 byte long and the additional prefetched instruction bytes are never used.

A memory interface with a bus width greater than one byte adds an artificial boundary to the instruction stream. For the purpose of this example, we are assuming a 4 byte memory interface. In this case we need an 8 byte prefetch buffer. On a branch to an address $address\ mod\ 4 > 4 - maximum\ instruction\ length$, two words need to be loaded from main memory before the processor can continue.

A memory technology, such as synchronous DRAM, has a large latency for the first accessed word and then a high bandwidth for the following words. Prefetching that only loads small quantities (one or two words) from the memory is therefore impracticable with these memory technologies.

Single Method Cache

A single method cache, although less efficient than a conventional instruction cache, can be incorporated very easily into the WCET analysis. The time needed for the memory transfer must be added to the invoke and return instructions.

The method cache also simplifies the hardware of the cache, as it means that no tag memory or address translation is necessary. Other parts of the processor are also smaller. The program counter, the associated adders and multiplexer are shorter than in a standard cache solution. For example, for a 1KB cache, the size of these units is only 10 bits, instead of 32 bits.

The main disadvantage of this single method cache is the high overhead when a complete method is loaded into the cache and only a small fraction of the code is executed. This issue is similar to that encountered with unused data in a cache line. However, in extreme cases, this overhead can be very high. The second problem can be seen in following example:

```
foo() {
    a();
    b();
}
```

This code sequence results in the following cache loads:

1. method foo is loaded on invocation of foo()

2. method a is loaded on invocation of a()

3. method foo is loaded on return from a()

4. method b is loaded on invocation of b()

5. method foo is loaded on return from b()

The main drawback of the single method cache is the multiple cache fill of foo() on return from methods a() and b(). In a conventional cache design, if these three methods fit in the cache memory at the same time and there is no placement conflict, each method is only loaded once. This issue can be overcome by caching more than one method. The simplest solution is a two-block cache.

Two-Block Cache

The two-block cache can hold up to two methods in the cache. This results in having to decide which block is replaced on a cache miss. With only two blocks, Least-Recently Used (LRU) is trivial to implement. The code sequence now results in the cache loads and hits as shown in Table 5.14. With the two-block cache, we have to double the cache memory or use both blocks for a single large method. The WCET analysis is slightly more complex than with a single block. A short history of the invocation sequence has to be used to find the cache fills and hits.

However, a cache that can only hold two methods is still very restrictive. The next code sequence shows the conflict. Table 5.15 shows the resulting cache loads.

Instruction	Block 1	Block 2	Cache
foo()	foo	–	load
a()	foo	a	load
return	foo	a	hit
b()	foo	b	load
return	foo	b	hit

Table 5.14: Cache load and hit example with the two-block cache

```
foo() {
    a();
}
a() {
    b();
}
```

Instruction	Block 1	Block 2	Cache
foo()	foo	–	load
a()	foo	a	load
b()	b	a	load
return	b	a	hit
return	foo	a	load

Table 5.15: Cache conflict example with the two-block cache

A memory (similar to the tag memory) with one word per block is used to store a reference to the cached method. However, this memory can be slower than the tag memory as it is only accessed on invocation or return, rather than on every cache access.

More Blocks

We can improve the hit rate by adding more blocks to the cache. If only one block per method is used, the cache size increases with the number of blocks. With more than two blocks, LRU replacement policy means that another word is needed for every block containing a use counter that is updated on every invoke and return. During replacement, this list is searched for the LRU block. Hit detection involves a search through the list of the method references of the blocks. If this search is done in

```
a() {
    for (;;) {
        b();
        c();
    }
    ...
}
```

Listing 5.8: Code fragment for the replacement example

microcode, it imposes a limit on the maximum number of blocks.

Variable Block Cache

Several cache blocks, all of the size as the largest method, are a waste of cache memory. Using smaller block sizes and allowing a method to span over several blocks, the blocks become very similar to cache lines. The main difference from a conventional cache is that the blocks for a method are all loaded at once and need to be consecutive.

Choosing the block size is now a major design decision. Smaller block sizes allow better memory usage, but the search time for a hit also increases.

With varying block numbers per method, an LRU replacement becomes impractical. When the method found to be LRU is smaller than the loaded method, this new method invalidates two cached methods.

For the replacement, we will use a pointer *next* that indicates the start of the blocks to be replaced on a cache miss. Two practical replace policies are:

Next block: At the very first beginning, *next* points to the first block. When a method of length l is loaded into the block n, *next* is updated to $(n+l)$ *mod block count*.

Stack oriented: *next* is updated in the same way as before on a method load. It is also updated on a method return – independent of a resulting hit or miss – to point to the first block of the leaving method.

We will show the operation of these different replacement policies in an example with three methods: a(), b() and c() of block sizes 2, 2 and 1. The cache consists of 4 blocks and is therefore too small to hold all the methods during the execution of the code fragment shown in Listing 5.8.   Tables 5.16 and 5.17 show the cache content during program execution for both replacement policies. The content of the cache blocks is shown after the execution of the invoke or return instruction. An uppercase letter indicates that this block has been newly loaded. A right arrow depicts the block

	a()	b()	ret	c()	ret	b()	ret	c()	ret	b()	ret
Block 1	A	→a	→a	C	c	B	b	b	→-	B	b
Block 2	A	a	a	→-	A	→a	→a	C	c	B	b
Block 3	→-	B	b	b	A	a	a	→-	A	→a	→a
Block 4	-	B	b	b	→-	B	b	b	A	a	a
Fill		2	4		5	7	9		11	13	15

Table 5.16: Next block replacement policy

	a()	b()	ret	c()	ret	b()	ret	c()	ret	b()	ret
Block 1	A	→a	a	a	a	→a	a	a	a	→a	a
Block 2	A	a	a	a	a	a	a	a	a	a	a
Block 3	→-	B	→b	C	→c	B	→b	C	→c	B	→b
Block 4	-	B	b	→-	-	B	b	→-	-	B	b
Fill		2	4		5		7		8		10

Table 5.17: Stack oriented replacement policy

to be replaced on a cache miss (the *next* pointer). The last row shows the number of blocks that are filled during the execution of the program.

In this example, the stack oriented approach needs fewer fills, as only methods b() and c() are exchanged and method a() stays in the cache. However, if, for example, method b() is the size of one block, all methods can be held in the cache using the the *next block* policy, but b() and c() would be still exchanged using the *stack* policy. Therefore, the first approach is used in the proposed cache.

5.8.3 WCET Analysis

The proposed instruction cache is designed to simplify WCET analysis. Due to the fact that all cache misses are only included in two instructions (*invoke* and *return*), the instruction cache can be ignored on all other instructions. The time needed to load a complete method is calculated using the memory properties (latency and bandwidth) and the length of the method. On an invoke, the length of the invoked method is used, and on a return, the method length of the caller is used to calculate the load time.

With a single method cache this calculation can be further simplified. For every invoke there is a corresponding return. That means that the time needed for the cache load on return can be included in the time for the invoke instruction. This is simpler because both methods, the caller and the callee, are known at the occurrence of the invoke instruction. The information about which method was the caller need not be stored for the return instruction to be analyzed.

With more than one method in the cache, a cache hit detection has to be performed as part of the WCET analysis. If there are only two blocks, this is trivial, as (i) a hit on invoke is only possible if the method is the same as the last invoked (e.g. a single method in a loop) and (ii) a hit on return is only possible when the method is a leaf in the call tree. In the latter case, it is always a hit.

When the cache contains more blocks (i.e. more than two methods can be cached), a part of the call tree has to be taken into account for hit detection. The variable block cache further complicates the analysis, as the method length also determines the cache content. However, this analysis is still simpler than a cache modeling of a direct-mapped instruction cache, as cache block replacement depends on the call tree instead of instruction addresses.

In traditional caches, data access and instruction cache fill requests can compete for the main memory bus. For example, a load or store at the end of the processor pipeline competes with an instruction fetch that results in a cache miss. One of the two instructions is stalled for additional cycles by the other instruction. With a data cache, this situation can be even worse. The worst-case scenario for the memory stall time for an instruction fetch or a data load is two miss penalties when both cache reads are a miss. This unpredictable behavior leads to very pessimistic WCET bounds.

A *method cache*, with cache fills only on invoke and return, does not interfere with data access to the main memory. Data in the main memory is accessed with *getfield* and *putfield*, instructions that never overlap with *invoke* and *return*. This property removes another uncertainty found in traditional cache designs.

5.8.4 Caches Compared

In this section, we will compare the different cache architectures in a quantitative way. Although our primary concern is predictability, performance remains important. We will therefore first present the results from a conventional direct-mapped instruction cache. These measurements will then provide a baseline for the evaluation of the proposed architecture.

Cache performance varies with different application domains. As the proposed system is intended for real-time applications, the benchmark for these tests should reflect this fact. However, there are no standard benchmarks available for embedded real-time systems. A real-time application was therefore adapted to create this benchmark. The application is from one node of a distributed motor control system

Cache size	Block size	MBIB	MTIB
1 KB	8	0.28	0.035
1 KB	16	0.38	0.024
1 KB	32	0.58	0.018
2 KB	8	0.17	0.022
2 KB	16	0.25	0.015
2 KB	32	0.41	0.013
4 KB	8	0.00	0.001
4 KB	16	0.01	0.000
4 KB	32	0.01	0.000

Table 5.18: Direct-mapped cache

[83] (see also Section 7.5.1). A simulation of the environment (sensors and actors) and the communication system (commands from the master station) forms part of the benchmark for simulating the real-world workload.

The data for all measurements was captured using a simulation of JOP and running the application for 500,000 clock cycles. During this time, the major loop of the application was executed several hundred times, effectively rendering any misses during the initialization code irrelevant to the measurements.

Direct-Mapped Cache

Table 5.18 gives the memory bytes and memory transactions per instruction byte for a standard direct-mapped cache. As we can see from the values for a cache size of 4KB, the kernel of the application is small enough to fit completely into the 4KB cache. The cache performs better (i.e. fewer bytes are transferred) with smaller block sizes. With smaller block sizes, the chance of unused data being read is reduced and the larger number of blocks reduces conflict misses. However, reducing the block size also increases memory transactions (MTIB), which directly relates to memory latency.

Which configuration performs best depends on the relationship between memory bandwidth and memory latency. Examples of average memory access times in cycles per instruction byte for different memory technologies are provided in Table 5.19. The third column shows the cache performance for a Static RAM (SRAM) that is very common in embedded systems. A latency of 1 clock cycle and an access time of 2 clock cycles per 32-bit word are assumed. For the synchronous DRAM (SDRAM) in the forth column, a latency of 5 cycles (3 cycle for the row address and 2 cycle

Cache size	Block size	SRAM	SDRAM	DDR
1 KB	8	**0.18**	0.25	0.19
1 KB	16	0.22	**0.22**	0.16
1 KB	32	0.31	0.24	**0.15**
2 KB	8	**0.11**	0.15	0.12
2 KB	16	0.14	**0.14**	**0.10**
2 KB	32	0.22	0.17	0.11

Table 5.19: Direct-mapped cache, average memory access time

CAS latency) is assumed. The memory delivers one word (4 bytes) per cycle. The Double Data Rate (DDR) SDRAM in the last column has an enhanced latency of 4.5 cycles and transfers data on both the rising and falling edge of the clock signal.

The data in bold give the best block size for different memory technologies. As expected, memories with a higher latency and bandwidth perform better with larger block sizes. For small block sizes, the latency clearly dominates the access time. Although the SRAM has half the bandwidth of the SDRAM and a quarter of the DDR, with a block size of 8 bytes, it is faster than the DRAM memories. In most cases a block size of 16 bytes is the fastest solution and we will therefore use this configuration for comparison with the following cache solutions.

Fixed Block Cache

Cache performance for single method per block architectures is shown in Table 5.20. The measurements for a simple 8 byte prefetch queue are also given, for reference. With prefetching, we would expect to see an MBIB of about 1. The 37% overhead results from the fact that the prefetch queue fetches 4 bytes a time and has to buffer a minimum of 3 bytes for the instruction fetch stage. On a branch or return, the queue is flushed and these bytes are lost.

A single block that has to be filled on every invoke and return requires considerable overheads. More than twice the amount of data is read from the main memory than is consumed by the processor. However, the memory transaction count is 16 times lower than with simple prefetching, which can compensate for the large MBIB for main memories with high latency.

The solution with two blocks for two methods performs almost twice as well as the simple one method cache. This is due to the fact that, for all leaves in the call tree, the caller method can be found on return. If the block count is doubled again, the number of misses is reduced by a further 25%, but the cache size also doubles.

Type	Cache size	MBIB	MTIB
Prefetch	8 B	1.37	0.342
Single method	1 KB	2.32	0.021
Two blocks	2 KB	1.21	0.013
Four blocks	4 KB	0.90	0.010

Table 5.20: Fixed block cache

Type	Cache size	SRAM	SDRAM	DDR
Prefetch	8 B	1.02	2.05	1.71
Single Method	1 KB	1.18	0.69	0.39
Two blocks	2 KB	0.62	0.37	0.21
Four blocks	4 KB	0.46	0.27	0.16

Table 5.21: Fixed block cache, average memory access time

For this measurement, an LRU replacement policy applies for the two and four block caches.

The same memory parameters as in the previous section are also used in Table 5.21. With the high latency of the DRAMs, even the simple one block cache is a faster (and more accurately predictable) solution than a prefetch queue. As MBIB and MTBI show the same trend as a function of the number of blocks, this is reflected in the access time in all three memory examples.

Variable Block Cache

Table 5.22 shows the cache performance of the proposed solution, i.e. of a method cache with several blocks per method, for different cache sizes and number of blocks. For this measurement, a *next block* replacement policy applies.

In this scenario, as the MBIB is very high at a cache size of 1KB and almost independent of the block count, the cache capacity is seen to be clearly dominant. The most interesting cache size with this benchmark is 2KB. Here, we can see the influence of the number of blocks on both performance parameters. Both values benefit from more blocks. However, a higher block count requires more time or more hardware for the hit detection. With a cache size of 4KB and enough blocks, the kernel of the application completely fits into the variable block cache, as we have seen with a 4KB traditional cache. From the gap between 16 and 32 blocks (within the 4KB cache), we can say that the application consists of fewer than 32 different

Cache size	Block count	MBIB	MTIB
1 KB	8	0.80	0.009
1 KB	16	0.71	0.008
1 KB	32	0.70	0.008
1 KB	64	0.70	0.008
2 KB	8	0.73	0.008
2 KB	16	0.37	0.004
2 KB	32	0.24	0.003
2 KB	64	0.12	0.001
4 KB	8	0.73	0.008
4 KB	16	0.25	0.003
4 KB	32	0.01	0.000
4 KB	64	0.00	0.000

Table 5.22: Variable block cache

methods.

It can be seen that even the smallest configuration with a cache size of 1KB and only 8 blocks outperforms fixed block caches with 2 or 4KB in both parameters (MBIB and MTIB). Compared with the fixed block solutions, MTIB is low in all configurations. This is due to the better hit rate, as indicated by the lower MBIB.

In most configurations, MBIB is higher than for the direct-mapped cache. It is very interesting to note that, in all configurations (even the small 1KB cache), MTIB is lower than in all 1KB and 2KB configurations of the direct-mapped cache. This is a result of the complete method transfers when a miss occurs and is clearly an advantage for main memory systems with high latency.

As in the previous examples, Table 5.23 shows the average memory access time per instruction byte for three different main memories.

In the DRAM configurations, the variable block cache directly benefits from the low MTBI. When comparing the values between SDRAM and DDR, we can see that the bandwidth affects the memory access time in a way that is approximately linear. The high latency of these memories is completely hidden. The configuration with 16 or more blocks and dynamic RAMs outperforms the direct-mapped cache of the same size. As expected, a memory with low latency (the SRAM in this example) depends on the MBIB values. The variable block cache is slower than the direct-mapped cache in the 1KB configuration because of the higher MBIB (0.7 compared to 0.3-0.6), and performs very similarly at a cache size of 2KB.

In Table 5.24, the different cache solutions with a size of 2KB are summarized.

Cache size	Block count	SRAM	SDRAM	DDR
1 KB	8	0.41	0.24	0.14
1 KB	16	0.36	0.22	0.12
1 KB	32	0.36	0.21	0.12
1 KB	64	0.36	0.21	0.12
2 KB	8	0.37	0.22	0.13
2 KB	16	0.19	0.11	0.06
2 KB	32	0.12	0.08	0.04
2 KB	64	0.06	0.04	0.02

Table 5.23: Variable block cache, average memory access time

Cache type	MBIB	MTIB
Single method	2.32	0.021
Two blocks	1.21	0.013
Variable block (16)	0.37	0.004
Variable block (32)	0.24	0.003
Direct-mapped	0.25	0.015

Table 5.24: Caches compared

The detail results of all caches can be found in Appendix E. All full method caches with two or more blocks have a lower MTIB than a conventional cache solution. This becomes more significant with increasing latency in main memories. The MBIB value is only quite high for one or two methods in the cache. However, the most surprising result is that the variable block cache with 32 blocks outperforms a direct-mapped cache of the same size at both values.

We can see that predictability is indirectly related to performance – a trend we had anticipated. The most predictable solution with a single method cache performs very poorly compared to a conventional direct-mapped cache. If we accept a slightly more complex WCET analysis (taking a small part of the call tree into account), we can use the two-block cache that is about two times better.

With the variable block cache, it could be argued that the WCET analysis becomes too complex, but it is nevertheless simpler than that with the direct-mapped cache. However, every hit in the two-block cache will also be a hit in a variable block cache (of the same size). A tradeoff might be to analyze the program by assuming a two-block cache but using a version of the variable block cache. The additional performance gain can than be used by non- or soft real-time parts of an application.

5.8.5 Summary

In this section, we have extended the single cache performance measurement *miss rate* to a two value set, memory read and transaction rate, in order to perform a more detailed evaluation of different cache architectures. From the properties of the Java language – usually small methods and relative branches – we derived the novel idea of a *method cache*, i.e. a cache organization in which whole methods are loaded into the cache on method invocation and the return from a method. This cache organization is time-predictable, as all cache misses are lumped together in these two instructions. Using only one block for a single method introduces considerable overheads in comparison with a conventional cache, but is very simple to analyze. We extended this cache to hold more methods, with one block per method and several smaller blocks per method.

Comparing these organizations quantitatively with a benchmark derived from a real-time application, we have seen that the variable block cache performs similarly to (and in one configuration even better than) a direct-mapped cache, in respect of the bytes that have to be filled on a cache miss. In all configurations and sizes of the variable block cache, the number of memory transactions, which relates to memory latency, is lower than in a traditional cache.

Only filling the cache on method invocation and return simplifies WCET analysis and removes another source of uncertainty, as there is no competition for the main memory access between instruction cache and data cache.

6 JOP Runtime System

A Java processor alone is not a complete JVM. This chapter describes the definition of a real-time profile for Java and a framework for a user-defined scheduler in Java. It concludes with the description of the JVM internal data structures to represent classes and objects.

6.1 A Real-Time Profile for Embedded Java

As standard Java is under-specified for real-time systems and the RTSJ does not fit for small embedded systems a new and simpler real-time profile is defined in this section and implemented on JOP. The guidelines of the specification are:

- High-integrity profile

- Easy syntax, simplicity

- Easy to implement

- Low runtime overhead

- No syntactic extension of Java

- Minimum change of Java semantics

- Support for time measurement if a WCET analysis tool is not available

- Known overheads (documentation of runtime behavior and memory requirements of every JVM operation and all methods have to be provided)

The real-time profile under discussion is inspired by the restricted versions of the RTSJ described in [79] and [56] (see Section 4.4.5). It is intended for high-integrity real-time applications and as a test case to evaluate the architecture of JOP as a Java processor for real-time systems.

The proposed definition is not compatible with the RTSJ. Since the application domain for the RTSJ is different from high-integrity systems, it makes sense for it *not* to be compatible with the RTSJ. Restrictions can be enforced by defining new classes (e.g. setting thread priority in the constructor of a real-time thread alone, enforcing minimum interarrival times for sporadic events).

All hardware interrupts are represented by threads under the control of the scheduler. With this solution, a priority is assigned to the device drivers and the execution time can be incorporated in the schedulability analysis with normal tasks. This solution also avoids problems with preemption latency provoked by device drivers. One example of this problem is the *caps-lock* issue in Linux [59]: A device driver performs a spinlock wait for keyboard acknowledgement and produces preemption latency up to $9166\mu s$. With the proposed concept of hardware interrupts under scheduler control, a lower assigned priority to such a device driver avoids preemption delays of *more important* real-time threads and events.

To verify that this specification is expressive enough for high-integrity real-time applications, Ravenscar-Java (RJ) [56] (see Section 4.4.5), with the additional necessary RTSJ classes, has been implemented on top of it. However, RJ inherits some of the complexity of the RTSJ. Therefore, the implementation of RJ has a larger memory and runtime overhead than this simple specification.

6.1.1 Application Structure

The application is divided in two different phases: *initialization* and *mission*. All non time-critical initialization, global object allocations, thread creation and startup are performed in the initialization phase. All classes need to be loaded and initialized in this phase. The mission phase starts after invocation of startMission(). The number of threads is fixed and the assigned priorities remain unchanged. The following restrictions apply to the application:

- Initialization and mission phase

- Fixed number of threads

- Threads are created at initialization phase

- All shared objects are allocated at initialization

6.1.2 Threads

Concurrency is expressed with two types of *schedulable objects*:

Periodic activities are represented by threads that execute in an infinite loop invoking waitForNextPeriod() to get rescheduled in predefined time intervals.

Asynchronous sporadic activities are represented by event handlers. Each event handler is in fact a thread, which is released by an hardware interrupt or a software generated event (invocation of fire()). Minimum interarrival time has to be specified on creation of the event handler.

The classes that implement the *schedulable objects* are:

RtThread represents a periodic task. As usual task work is coded in run(), which gets invoked on missionStart(). A scoped memory object can be attached to an RtThread at creation.

HwEvent represents an interrupt with a minimum interarrival time. If the hardware generates more interrupts, they get lost.

SwEvent represents a software-generated event. It is triggered by fire() and needs to override handle().

Listing 6.1 shows the definition of the basic classes.

Listing 6.2 shows the principle coding of a worker thread. An example for creation of two real-time threads and an event handler can be seen in Listing 6.3.

6.1.3 Scheduling

The scheduler is a preemptive, priority-based scheduler with unlimited priority levels and a unique priority value for each schedulable object. No real-time threads or events are scheduled during the initialization phase.

The design decision to use unique priority levels, instead of FIFO within priorities, is based on following facts: Two common ways to assign priorities are rate monotonic and, in a more general form, deadline monotonic assignment. When two tasks are given the same priority, we can choose one of them and assign a higher priority to that task and the task set will still be schedulable. This results in a strictly monotonic priority order and we do not need to deal with FIFO order. This eliminates queues for each priority level and results in a single, priority ordered task list with unlimited priority levels.

Synchronized blocks are executed with priority ceiling emulation protocol. An object, used for synchronization, for which the priority is not set, top priority is assumed. This avoids priority inversions on objects that are not accessible from the application (e.g. objects inside a library).

In addition, the scheduler contains methods for worst-case time measurement for both the periodic work and handler methods. These measured execution times can be used during development when no WCET analysis tool is available.

```java
public class RtThread {

    public RtThread(int priority, int period)
    public RtThread(int priority, int period, int offset)
    public RtThread(int priority, int period, Memory mem)
    public RtThread(int priority, int period, int offset,
                 Memory mem)

    public void enterMemory()
    public void exitMemory()

    public void run()
    public boolean waitForNextPeriod()

    public static void startMission()
}

public class HwEvent extends RtThread {

    public HwEvent(int priority, int minTime, int number)
    public HwEvent(int priority, int minTime, Memory mem,
                 int number)

    public void handle()
}

public class SwEvent extends RtThread {

    public SwEvent(int priority, int minTime)
    public SwEvent(int priority, int minTime, Memory mem)

    public final void fire()
    public void handle()
}
```

Listing 6.1: Schedulable objects

6.1.4 Memory

The profile does not support a garbage collector. All memory should be allocated at the initialization phase. Without a garbage collector, the heap implicitly becomes immortal memory (as defined by the RTSJ). For objects created during the mission phase, a scoped memory is provided. Each scoped memory area is assigned to one RtThread. A scoped memory area cannot be shared between threads. No references are allowed from the heap to scoped memory. Scoped memory is explicitly entered and left using invocations from the application logic. Memory areas are cleared both on creation and when leaving the scope (invocation of exitMemory()), leading to a memory area with constant allocation time, as opposed to memory with linear allocation time (as the memory type LTMemory in the RTSJ) [21].

6.1.5 Restriction of Java

A list of some of the language features that should be avoided for WCET analyzable real-time threads and bound memory usage:

WCET: Only analyzable language constructs are allowed (see [78]).

Static class initialization: Since the definition when to call the static class initializer is problematic (see Section 4.2), they are disallowed. Move this code to a static method (e.g. init()) and invoke it explicit in the initialization phase.

Inheritance: Reduce usage of interfaces and overridden methods.

String concatenation: In immortal memory scope only string concatenation with string literals is allowed.

Finalization: finalize() has a weak definition in Java. Because real-time systems run *forever*, objects in the heap, which is immortal in this specification, will never be finalized. Objects in scoped memory are released on exitMemory(). However, finalizations on these objects complicate WCET analysis of exitMemory().

Dynamic Class Loading: Due to the implementation and WCET analysis complexity dynamic class loading is avoided.

A program analysis tool can greatly help in enforcing these restrictions.

```
public class Worker extends RtThread {

    private SwEvent event;

    public Worker(int p, int t,
                    SwEvent ev) {

        super(p, t,
            // create a scoped memory area
            new Memory(10000)
        );
        event = ev;
        init();
    }

    private void init() {
        // all initialzation stuff
        // has to be placed here
    }

    public void run() {

        for (;;) {
            work();        // do some work
            event.fire(); // and fire an event

            // some work in scoped memory
            enterMemory();
            workWithMem();
            exitMemory();

            // wait for next period
            if (!waitForNextPeriod()) {
                missedDeadline();
            }
        }
        // should never reach this point
    }
}
```

Listing 6.2: A periodic real-time thread

```
// create an Event
Handler h = new Handler(3, 1000);

// create two worker threads with
// priorities according to their periods
FastWorker fw = new FastWorker(2, 2000);
Worker w = new Worker(1, 10000, h);

// change to mission phase for all
// periodic threads and event handler
RtThread.startMission();

// do some non real-time work
// and invoke sleep() or yield()
for (;;) {
    watchdogBlink();
    Thread.sleep(500);
}
```

Listing 6.3: Start of the application

6.1.6 Implementation Results

The initial idea was to implement scheduling and dispatching in microcode. However, many Java bytecodes have a one to one mapping to a microcode instruction, resulting in a single cycle execution. The performance gain of an algorithm coded in microcode is therefore negligible. As a result, almost all of the scheduling is implemented in Java. Only a small part of the dispatcher, a memory copy, is implemented in microcode and exposed with a special bytecode.

Experimental results of basic scheduling benchmarks, such as periodic thread jitter, context switch time for threads and asynchronous events, can be found in Section 7.3.2.

To implement system functions, such as scheduling, in Java, access to JVM and processor internal data structures have to be available. However, Java does not allow memory access or access to hardware devices. In JOP, this access is provided by way of additional bytecodes. In the Java environment, these bytecodes are represented as static native methods. The compiled invoke instruction for these methods (invokestatic) is replaced by these additional bytecodes in the class file. This solution provides a very efficient way to incorporate low-level functions into a pure Java system. The translation can be performed during class loading to avoid non-standard class files.

A pure Java system, without an underlying RTOS, is an unusual system with some interesting new properties. Java is a safer execution environment than C (e.g. no pointers) and the boundary between *kernel* and *user space* can become quite loose. Scheduling, usually part of the operating system or the JVM, is implemented in Java and executed in the same context as the application. This property provides an easy path to a framework for user-defined scheduling.

6.2 User-Defined Scheduler

The novel approach to implement a real-time scheduler in Java opens up new possibilities. An obvious next step is to extend this system to provide a framework for user-defined scheduling in Java. New applications, such as multimedia streaming, result in *soft* real-time systems that need a more flexible scheduler than the traditional fixed priority based ones. This section provides a simple-to-use framework to evaluate new scheduling concepts for these applications in real-time Java.

The following section analyzes which events are exposed to the scheduler and which functions from the JVM need to be available in the user space. It is followed by the definition of the framework and examples of how to implement a scheduler using this framework.

6.2.1 Schedule Events

The most important element of the user-defined scheduler is to define which events result in the scheduling of a new task. When such an event occurs, the user-defined scheduler is invoked. It can update its task list and decide which task is dispatched.

Timer interrupt: For timed scheduling decisions, a programmable timer generates exact timed interrupts. The scheduler controls the time interval for the next interrupt.

HW interrupt: Each hardware-generated interrupt can be associated with an asynchronous event. This allows the execution of a device driver under the control of the scheduler. Latencies of the device driver can be controlled by assigning the right priority in a priority scheduler.

Monitor: To allow different implementations of priority inversion protocols, hooks for monitorenter and monitorexit are provided.

Thread block: Each thread can cease execution via a call of the scheduler. This function is used to implement methods such as waitForNextPeriod() or sleep(). The reason for blocking (e.g. end of periodic work) has to be communicated to the scheduler (e.g. next time to be unblocked for a periodic task).

SW event: Invoking fire() on an event provides support for signaling. wait(), notify() or notifyAll() are not necessary. However, this mechanism is not part of the scheduling framework. It can be implemented with the user-defined scheduler and an associated thread class.

6.2.2 Data Structures

To implement a scheduler in Java, some JVM internal data structures need to be accessible.

Object: In Java, any object (including an object from the class Class for static methods) can be used for synchronization. Different priority inversion protocols require different data structures to be associated with an object. Each object provides a field, accessed through a Scheduler method, in which these data structures can be attached.

Thread: A list of all threads is provided to the scheduler. The scheduler is also notified when a new thread object is created or a thread terminates. The scheduler controls the start of threads.

6.2.3 Services for the Scheduler

The real-time JVM and the hardware platform have to provide some minimum services. These services are exposed through Scheduler:

Dispatch: The current active thread is interrupted and a new thread is placed in the run state.

Time: System time with high resolution (microseconds, if the hardware can provide it) is used for time derived scheduling decisions.

Timer: A programmable timer interrupt (not a timer tick) is necessary for accurate time triggered scheduling.

Interrupts: To protect the data structures of the scheduler all interrupts can be disabled and enabled.

6.2.4 Class Scheduler

The class Scheduler has to be extended to implement a user-defined scheduler. The class Task represents *schedulable objects*. For non-trivial scheduling algorithms, Task is also extended. The scheduler lives in normal thread space. There is no special context such as kernel space. The methods of Scheduler are categorized by the caller module and described in detail below.

Application   To use a scheduler in an application, the application only has to create one instance of the scheduler class and has to decide when scheduling starts.

```
public Scheduler()
```

A single instance of the scheduler is created by the application.

```
public void start()
```

This method initiates the transition to the mission phase of the application. All created tasks are started and scheduled under the control of the user scheduler.

Task   A user-defined scheduler usually needs an associated user-defined thread class (an extension of Task). This class interacts with the scheduler by invoking following methods from Scheduler:

```
void addTask(Task t)
```

The scheduler has access to the list of created tasks to use at the start of scheduling. For dynamic task creation after the start of the scheduler, this method is called by the constructor of Task, to notify the scheduler to update its list.

void **isDead**(Task t)

The scheduler is notified when a Task returns from the run() method. The scheduler removes this Task from the list of schedulable objects.

void **block**()

Every Task can cease execution via a call of the scheduler. This method is used to implement methods such as waitForNextPeriod() or sleep() in a user defined thread class.

Java Virtual Machine   The methods listed below provide the essential points of communication between the JVM and the scheduler. As a response to an interrupt (hardware or timer), entrance or exit of a synchronized method/block the JVM invokes a method from the scheduler.

abstract void **schedule**()

This is the main entry point for the scheduler. This method has to be overridden to implement the scheduling algorithm. It is called from the JVM on a timed event or a software interrupt (see genInt()) is issued (e.g. when a Task gives up execution).

void **interrupt**(int nr)

The scheduler is notified on a hardware event. It can directly call an associated device driver or use this information to unblock a waiting task.

void **monitorEnter**(Object o)
void **monitorExit**(Object o)

These methods are invoked by the JVM on synchronized methods and blocks (JVM bytecodes monitorenter and monitorexit). They provide hooks for executing dynamic priority changes in the scheduler.

Scheduler   Services of the JVM needed to implement a scheduler are provided through static methods.

static final void **genInt**()

This service from the JVM schedules a software interrupt. As a result, schedule() is called. This method is the standard way of switching control to the scheduler. It is e.g. invoked by block().

```
static final void enableInt()
static final void disableInt()
```

The scheduler cannot use monitors to protect its data structures as the scheduler itself is in charge of handling monitors. To protect the data structures of the scheduler, it can globally enable and disable interrupts.

```
static final void dispatch(Task nextTask, int nextTim)
```

This method dispatches a Task and schedules a timer interrupt at nextTim.

```
static final void attachData(Object obj, Object data)
static final Object getAttachedData(Object obj)
```

The behavior of the priority inversion avoidance protocol is defined by the user scheduler. The root of the Java class hierarchy (java.lang.Object) contains a JVM internal reference of generic type Object that can be used by the scheduler to attach data structures for monitors. The first argument of these methods is the object that is used as monitor.

Scheduler or Task   The following two methods are utility functions useful for the scheduler and the thread implementation.

```
static final int getNow()
```

To support time-triggered scheduling, the system provides access to a high-resolution time or counter. The returned value is the time since startup in microseconds. The exact resolution is implementation-dependent.

```
static final Task getRunningTask()
```

The current running Task (in which context the scheduler is called) is returned by this method.

6.2.5 Class Task

A basic structure for schedulable objects is shown in Listing 6.4. This class is usually extended to provide a thread implementation that fits to the user-defined scheduler. The class Task is intended to be minimal. To avoid inheriting methods that do not fit for some applications, it does not extend java.lang.Thread. However, Task can be used to *implement* java.lang.Thread.

The methods enterMemory and exitMemory are used by the application to provide scoped memory for temporary allocated objects. Task provides a list of active tasks for the scheduler.

```
public class Task {

    public Task()
    public Task(Memory mem)
    void start()

    public void enterMemory()
    public void exitMemory()

    public void run()

    static Task getFirstTask()
    static Task getNextTask()
}
```

Listing 6.4: A basic schedulable object

One issue, raised by the implementation of the framework is the way in which access rights to methods need to be defined in Java. All methods, except `start()`, should be `private` or `protected`. However, some methods, such as `schedule()`, are invoked by a part of the JVM, which is also written in Java but resides in a different package. This results in defining the methods as public and *hoping* that they are not invoked by the application code. The C++ concept of friends would greatly help in sharing information over package boundaries without making this information public.

6.2.6 A Simple Example Scheduler

Listing 6.5 shows a full example of using this framework to implement a simple round robin scheduler.

The only method that needs to be supplied is `schedule()`. For a more advanced scheduler, it is necessary to provide a combination of a user defined thread class and a scheduler class. These two classes have to be tightly integrated, as the scheduler uses information provided by the thread objects for its scheduling decisions.

```java
public class RoundRobin extends Scheduler {

    //
    //   test threads
    //
    static class Work extends Task {

        private int c;

        Work(int ch) {
            c = ch;
        }

        public void run() {

            for (;;) {
                Dbg.wr(c); // debug output

                // busy wait to simulate
                // 3 ms workload in Work.
                int ts = Scheduler.getNow();
                ts += 3000;
                while (ts-Scheduler.getNow()>0)
                    ;
            }
        }
    }

    //
    //   user scheduler starts here
    //

    public void addTask(Task t) {
        // we do not allow tasks to be
        // added after start().
    }

    //
    //   called by the JVM
```

```
//
public void schedule() {
    Task t = getRunningTask().getNextTask();
    if (t==null) t = Task.getFirstTask();
    dispatch(t, getNow()+10000);
}


public static void main(String[] args) {

    new Work('a');
    new Work('b');
    new Work('c');

    RoundRobin rr = new RoundRobin();

    rr.start();
}
}
```

Listing 6.5: A very simple scheduler

6.2.7 Interaction of Task, Scheduler and the JVM

The framework is used to re-implement the scheduler described in Section 6.1. In the original implementation, the interaction between scheduling and threads was simple, as the scheduling was part of the thread class. Using the framework, these functions have to be split to two classes, extending Task and Scheduler. Both classes are placed in the same package to provide simpler information sharing with some protection from the rest of the application. For performance reasons data structures are directly exposed from one class to the other.

The resulting implementation is compatible with the first definition, with the exception that RtThread now extends Task. However, no changes in the application code are necessary.

Figure 6.1 is an interaction example of this scheduler within the framework. The interaction diagram shows the message sequences between two application tasks, the scheduler, the JVM and the hardware. The hardware represents interrupt and timer logic. The corresponding code fragments of the application, RtThread and PriorityScheduler are shown in Listing 6.6, 6.7 and 6.8. Task 2 is a periodic task with a higher priority than Task 1.

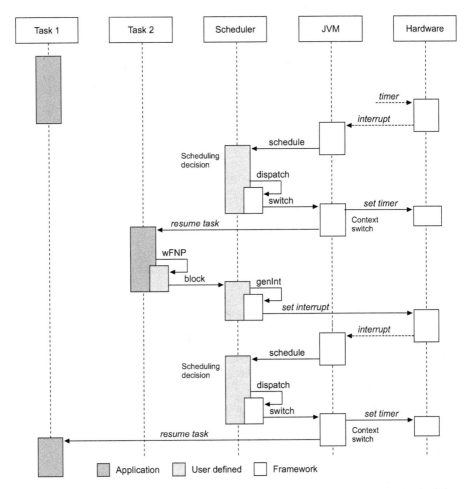

Figure 6.1: Interaction and message exchange between the application, the scheduler, the JVM and the hardware

```
for (;;) {
    doPeriodicWork();
    waitForNextPeriod();
}
```

Listing 6.6: Code fragment oft the application

The first event is a timer event to unblock Task 2 for a new period. The generated timer event results in a call of the user defined scheduler. The scheduler performs its scheduling decision and issues a context switch to Task 2. With every context switch the timer is reprogrammed to generate an interrupt at the next time triggered event for a higher priority task. Task 2 performs the periodic work and ceases execution by invocation of waitForNextPeriod(). The scheduler is called and requests an interrupt from the hardware resulting in the same call sequence as with a timer or other hardware interrupt. The software generated interrupt imposes negligible overhead and results in a single entry point for the scheduler. Task 1 is the only ready task in this example and is resumed by the scheduler.

Using a general scheduling framework for a real-time scheduler is not without its costs. Additional methods are invoked from a scheduling event until the actual dispatch takes place. The context switch is about 20% slower than in the original implementation. It is the opinion of the author that the additional cost is outweighed by the flexibility of the framework.

6.2.8 Predictability

The architecture of JOP is designed to simplify WCET analysis. Every JVM bytecode maps to one ore more microcode instructions. Every microcode instruction takes exactly one cycle to execute. Thus, the execution time at the bytecode level is known cycle accurately. The microcode contains no data dependent or unbound loops that would compromise the WCET analysis (see Section 7.4).

The worst-case time for dispatching is known cycle accurately on this architecture. Only the time behavior of the user scheduler needs to be analyzed. With the known WCET of every bytecode, as listed in Appendix D, the WCET of the scheduler can be obtained by examining it at the bytecode level. This can be done manually or with a WCET analysis tool.

```java
public boolean waitForNextPeriod() {

    synchronized(monitor) {

        // ps is the instance of
        // the PriorityScheduler
        int nxt = ps.next[nr] + period;

        int now = Scheduler.getNow()
        if (nxt—now < 0) {
            // missed deadline
            doMissAction();
            return false;
        } else {
            // time for the next unblock
            ps.next[nr] = nxt;
        }
        // just schedule an interrupt
        // schedule() gets called.
        ps.block();
    }
    return true;
}
```

Listing 6.7: Implementation in RtThread

```
public void schedule() {

    // Find the ready thread with
    // the highest priority.
    int nr = getReady();

    // Search the list of sleeping threads
    // to find the nearest release time
    // in the future of a higher priority
    // thread than the one that will be
    // released now.
    int time = getNextTimer(nr);

    // This time is used for the next
    // timer interrupt.
    // Perform the context switch.
    dispatch(task[nr], time);
    // No access to locals after this point.
    // We are running in the NEW context!
}
```

Listing 6.8: Implementation of the PriorityScheduler

6.2.9 Related Work

Several implementations of user-level schedulers in standard operating systems have been proposed. In [59], the Linux scheduling mechanism is enhanced. It is divided into a dispatcher and an allocator. The dispatcher remains in kernel space; while the allocator is implemented as a user space function. The allocator transforms four basic scheduling parameters (priority, start time, finish time and budget) into scheduling attributes to be used by the dispatcher. Many existing schedulers can be supported with this parameter set, but others that are based on different parameters cannot be implemented. This solution does not address the implementation of protocols for shared resources.

A different approach defines a new API to enable applications to use application-defined scheduling in a way compatible with the scheduling model defined in POSIX [82]. It is implemented in the MaRTE OS, a minimal real-time kernel that provides the C and Ada language POSIX interface. This interface has been submitted to the Real-Time POSIX Working Group for consideration.

One approach to user-level scheduling in Java can be found in [29]. A thread *multiplexor*, as part of the FLEX ahead-of-time compiler system for Java, is used for utility accrual scheduling. However, the underlying operating system – in this case Linux – can still be seen through the framework and there is no support for Java synchronization.

6.2.10 Summary

This section and Section 6.1 consider the implementation of real-time scheduling on a Java processor. The novelty of the described approach is in implementing functions usually associated with an RTOS in Java. That means that real-time Java is not based on an RTOS, and therefore not restricted to the functionality provided by the RTOS. With JOP, a self-contained real-time system in pure Java becomes possible. This system is augmented with a framework to provide scheduling functions at the application level. The implementation of the specification, described in Section 6.1, is successfully used as the basis for a commercial real-time application in the railway industry. Future work will extend this framework to support multiple schedulers. A useful combination of schedulers would be: one for standard java.lang.Thread (optimized for throughput), one for soft real-time tasks and one for hard real-time tasks.

6.3 JVM Architecture

This section presents the details of the implementation of the JVM on JOP. The representation of objects and the stack frame is chosen to support JOP as processor for real-time systems. However, since the data structures are realized through microcode they can be easily changed for a system with different needs. For example: to simplify a compacting GC a handle to an object can be implemented by changing the microcode of getfield, putfield and new.

6.3.1 Runtime Data Structures

Memory is addressed as 32-bit data, which means that memory pointers are incremented for every four bytes. No single byte or 16-bit access is necessary. The abstract type reference is a pointer to memory that represents the object or an array. The reference is pushed on the stack before an instruction can operate on it. A null reference is represented by the value 0.

Stack Frame

On invocation of a method, the invoker's context is saved in a newly allocated frame on the stack. It is restored when the method returns. The saved context consists of following registers:

SP: Immediately before invocation the stack pointer points to the last argument for the called function. This value is reduced by the argument count (i.e. the arguments are consumed) and saved in the new stack frame.

PC: The pointer to the next bytecode instruction after the invoke instruction.

VP: The pointer to the memory area on the stack that contains the locals.

CP: The pointer to the constant pool of the class from the invoking method.

MP: The pointer to the method structure of the invoking method.

SP, PC and VP are registers in JOP while CP and MP are local variables of the JVM. Figure 6.2 provides an example of the stack before and after invoking a method. In this example, the called method has two arguments and contains two local variables. If the method is a virtual one, the first argument is the reference to the object (the *this*-pointer). The arguments implicit become locals in the called method and are accessed in the same way as local variables. The start of the stack frame (*Frame* in the figure) needs not to be saved. It is not needed during execution of the method or

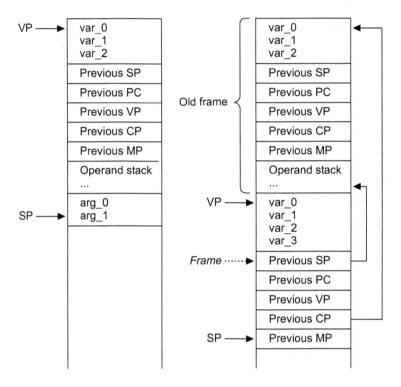

Figure 6.2: Stack change on method invocation

on return. To access the starting address of the frame (e.g. for an exception) it can be calculated with information from the method structure:

$$Frame = VP + arg\_cnt + locals\_cnt$$

Object Layout

Figure 6.3 shows the representation of an object in memory. The object reference points to the first instance variable of the object. At the offset -1, a pointer is located to access class information. To speed-up method invocation, it points directly to the method table of the objects class instead of the beginning of the class data.

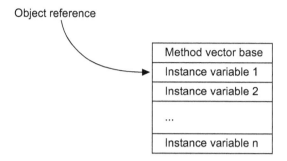

Figure 6.3: Object format

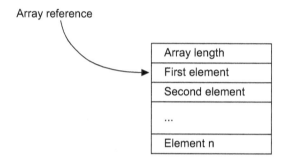

Figure 6.4: Array format

Array Layout

Figure 6.4 shows the representation of an array in memory. The object reference points to the first element of the array. At the offset -1, the length of the array can be found.

Class Structure

Runtime class information, as shown in Figure 6.5, consists of the class variables, the dispatch table for the methods, the constant pool and an optional interface table.

The class reference is obtained from the constant pool when a new object is created. The method vector base pointer is a reference from an object to its class (see Figure 6.3). It is used on invokevirtual with an index retrieved from the constant pool. A pointer to the method structure of the current method is saved in the JVM variable MP. The method structure, as shown in Figure 6.6, contains the starting address and length of the method (in 32-bit words), argument and local variable count

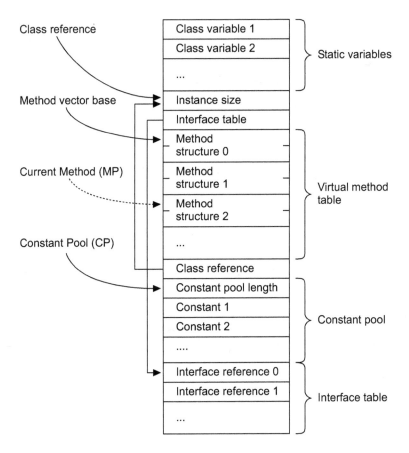

Figure 6.5: Runtime class structure

Start address	Method length	
Constant pool	Local count	Arg. count

Figure 6.6: Method structure

and a pointer to the constant pool of the class. Since the constant pool is an often accessed memory area, a pointer to it is kept in the JVM variable CP.

The interface table contains references to the method structures of the implementation. Only classes that implement an interface contain this table. To avoid searching the class hierarchy on invokeinterface, each interface method is assigned a unique index. This provides constant execution time, but can lead to large interface tables.

The constant pool contains various constants of a class. The entry at index 0 is the length of the pool. All constants, which are symbolic in the class files, are resolved on class loading or during pre-linking. The different constant types and their values after resolving are listed in Table 6.1. The names for the types are the same as in the JVM specification [60].

Constant type	Description
Class	A pointer to a class (class reference)
Fieldref	For static fields: a direct pointer to the field
	For object fields: the position relative to the object reference
Methodref	For static methods: a direct pointer to the method structure
	For virtual methods: the offset in the method table (= index*2) and the number of arguments
InterfaceMethodref	A system wide unique index into the interface table
String	A pointer to the string object that represents the string constant
Integer	The constant value
Float	The constant value
Long	This constant value spans two entries in the constant pool
Double	Same as for long constants
NameAndType	Not used
Utf8	Not used

Table 6.1: Constant pool entries

7 Results

In this chapter, we will present the evaluation results for JOP, with respect to size, performance and WCET. Table 7.1 compares JOP with other Java hardware solutions (see also Chapter 3). The column year indicates the first date at which the processor became available or the first publication about the processor. The research project Komodo has now ceased, while FemtoJava is still being used as a basis for active research.

We can see that JOP is the smallest realization in an FPGA and also has the highest clock frequency. JOP also has a minimum CPI of 1 while, for Komodo and Femto-Java, the minimum CPIs are four and three respectively.

	Target technology	Size	Speed [MHz]	Java standard	Min. CPI	Year
JOP	Altera, Xilinx FPGA	1830 LCs, 3KB RAM	100	J2ME CLDC	1	2001
picoJava	No realization	128K gates + memory		Full	1	1999
aJile	ASIC 0.25μ	25K gates + ROM	100	J2ME CLDC		2000
Moon	Altera FPGA	3660 LCs, 4KB RAM				2000
Lightfoot	Xilinx FPGA	3400 LCs	40			2001
Komodo	Xilinx FPGA	2600 LCs	33		4	2000
FemtoJava	Altera Flex 10K	2000 LCs	4	Subset: 69 bytecodes, 16-bit ALU	3	2001

Table 7.1: Comparison of Java hardware with JOP

In the following section, the hardware platform that is used for benchmarking is described. This is followed by a comparison of JOP's resource usage with other soft-core processors. In the 'General Performance' section, a number of different solutions for embedded Java are compared at the bytecode level and at the application level. The basic properties of the real-time scheduler are evaluated using the Reference Implementation (RI) of the RTSJ on a Linux system and the real-time profile from Section 6.1 on top of JOP. It is also shown that our objective of providing an easy target for WCET analysis has been achieved. This chapter concludes with a short description of real-world applications that use JOP.

7.1 Hardware Platforms

During the development of JOP and its predecessors, several different FPGA boards were developed. The first experiments involved using Altera FPGAs EPF8282, EPF8452, EPF10K10 and ACEX 1K30 on boards that were connected to the printer port of a PC for configuration, download and communication. The next step was the development of a stand-alone board with FLASH memory and static RAM. This board was developed in two variants, one with an ACEX 1K50 and the other with a Cyclone EP1C6 or EP1C12. Both boards are pin-compatible and are used in commercial applications of JOP. The Cyclone board is the hardware that is used for the following evaluations.

This board is an ideal development system for JOP. Static RAM and FLASH are connected via independent buses to the FPGA. All unused FPGA pins and the serial line are available via four connectors. The FLASH can be used to store configuration data for the FPGA and application program/data. The FPGA can be configured with a ByteBlasterMV download cable or loaded from the flash (with a small CPLD on board). As the FLASH is also connected to the FPGA, it can be programmed from the FPGA. This allows for upgrades of the Java program and even the processor core itself in the field. The board is slightly different from other FPGA prototyping boards, in that its connectors are on the bottom side. Therefore, it can be used as a module (60mm x 48mm), i.e. as part of a larger board that contains the periphery. The Cyclone board contains:

- Altera Cyclone EP1C6Q240 or EP1C12Q240

- Step Down voltage regulator (1V5)

- Crystal clock (20MHz) at the PLL input (up to 640MHz internal)

- 512KB FLASH (for FPGA configuration and program code)

- 1MB fast asynchronous RAM (15 ns)

- Up to 128MB NAND FLASH

- ByteBlasterMV port

- Watchdog with LED

- EPM7064 PLD to configure the FPGA from the FLASH on watchdog reset

- Serial interface driver (MAX3232)

- 56 general-purpose IO pins

The RAM consists of two independent 16-bit banks (with their own address and control lines). Both RAM chips are on the bottom side of the PCB, directly under the FPGA pins. As the traces are very short (under 10mm), it is possible to use the RAMs at full speed without reflection problems. The two banks can be combined to form 32-bit RAM or support two independent CPU cores. Pictures and the schematic of the board can be found in Appendix F.

An expansion board hosts the CPU module and provides a complete Java processor system with Internet connection. A step down switching regulator with a large AC/DC input range supplies the core board. All input and output pins are EMC/ESD-protected and routed to large connectors (5.08mm Phoenix). Analog comparators can be used to build sigma-delta ADCs. For FPGA projects with a network connection, a CS8900 Ethernet controller with an RJ45 connector is included on the expansion board.

7.2 Resource Usage

Cost, alongside energy consumption, is an important issue for embedded systems. The cost of a chip is directly related to the die size (the cost per die is roughly proportional to the square of the die area [40]). Chips with fewer gates also consume less energy. Processors for embedded systems are therefore optimized for minimum chip size. In this section, we will compare JOP with different processors in terms of size.

One major design objective in the development of JOP was to create a small system that could be implemented in a low-cost FPGA. Table 7.2 shows the resource usage for different configurations of JOP and different soft-core processors implemented in an Altera EP1C6 FPGA [16]. Estimating equivalent gate counts for designs in an FPGA is problematic. It is therefore better to compare the two basic structures, LC (logic cell) and memory.

Processor	Resources [LC]	Memory [KB]	fmax [MHz]
JOP Minimal	1,077	3.25	98
JOP Basic	1,452	3.25	98
JOP Typical	1,831	3.25	101
Lightfoot[1]	3,400	1	40
NIOS A	1,828	6.2	120
NIOS B	2,923	5.5	119
SPEAR[2]	1,700	8	80

Table 7.2: FPGA soft-core processors

All configurations of JOP contain a memory interface to a 32-bit static RAM and an 8-bit FLASH for the Java program and configuration data. The minimum configuration implements multiplication and the shift operations in microcode. In the basic configuration, these operations are implemented as a sequential Booth multiplier and a single-cycle barrel shifter. The typical configuration contains a variable block instruction cache (1KB, 4 blocks – see Section 5.8.2) and some useful I/O devices such as an UART and a timer with interrupt logic for multi-threading. The typical configuration of JOP needs about 30% of the LCs in a Cyclone EP1C6, thus leaving enough resources free for application-specific logic.

Lightfoot [62] is a commercial Java processor, targeted at Xilinx FPGA architectures. We can see from Table 7.2 that this processor needs about twice the resources of JOP.

As a reference, NIOS [15], Altera's popular RISC soft-core, is also included in the list. NIOS has a 16-bit instruction set, a 5-stage pipeline and can be configured with a 16 or 32-bit datapath. Version A is the minimum configuration of NIOS. Version B adds an external memory interface, multiplication support and a timer. Version A is comparable with the minimal configuration of JOP, and Version B with its typical configuration.

SPEAR [22] (Scalable Processor for Embedded Applications in Real-time Environments) is a 16-bit processor with deterministic execution times. SPEAR contains

---

[1] The data for the Lightfoot processor is taken from the data sheet [62]. The frequency used is that in a Vertex-II device from Xilinx. JOP can be clocked at 100MHz in the Vertex-II device, making this comparison valid.

[2] As SPEAR uses internal memory blocks in asynchronous mode it is not possible to synthesize it without modification for the Cyclone FPGA. The clock frequency of SPEAR in an Altera Cyclone is an estimate based on following facts: SPEAR can be clocked at 40MHz in an APEX device and JOP can be clocked at 50MHz in the same device.

Processor	Core [gate]	Memory [gate]	Sum. [gate]
JOP	11K	39K	50K
picoJava	128K	314K	442K
aJile	25K	912K	937K
Pentium MMX			1125K

Table 7.3: Gate count estimates for various processors

predicated instructions to support single-path programming. SPEAR is included in the list as it is also a processor designed for real-time systems.

To prove that the VHDL code for JOP is as portable as possible, JOP was also implemented in a Xilinx Spartan-3 FPGA. Only the instantiation and initialization code for the on-chip memories is vendor-specific, whilst the rest of the VHDL code can be shared for the different targets. JOP consumes about the same LC count (1844 LCs) in the Spartan device, but has a slower clock frequency (83MHz).

From this comparison we can see that we have achieved our objective of designing a small processor. The Java processor, Lightfoot, is 2.3 times larger (and 2.5 times slower) than JOP in the basic configuration. A typical 32-bit RISC processor consumes about 1.6 to 1.8 times the resources of JOP. However, the RISC processor can be clocked 20% faster than JOP in the same technology. The only processor that is similar in size is SPEAR. However, while SPEAR is a 16-bit processor, JOP contains a 32-bit datapath.

Table 7.3 provides gate count estimates for JOP, picoJava, the aJile processor, and the Intel Pentium MMX processor that is used in the benchmarks in the next section. Equivalent gate count for an LC[3] varies between 5.5 and 7.4 – we chose a factor of 6 gates per LC and 1.5 gates per memory bit for the estimated gate count for JOP in the table. JOP is listed in the typical configuration that consumes 1831 LCs. The Pentium MMX contains 4.5M transistors [26] that are equivalent to 1125K gates.

We can see from the table that the on-chip memory dominates the overall gate count of JOP, and to an even greater extent, of the aJile processor. The aJile processor is roughly the same size as the Pentium MMX, and both are about 20 times larger than JOP.

---

[3]The factors are derived from the data provided for various processors in Chapter 3 and from the resource estimates in Section 5.5.

7.3 Performance

In this section, we will evaluate the performance of JOP in relation to other Java systems. Although JOP is intended as a processor with a low WCET for all operations, its general performance is still important. In the first section, we will evaluate JOP's average performance.

In the section that follows it, the implementation of the simple real-time profile, as described in Section 6.1, on JOP is compared to the RI of the RTSJ on top of Linux.

7.3.1 General Performance

Running benchmarks is problematic, both generally and especially in the case of embedded systems. The best benchmark would be the application that is intended to run on the system being tested. To get comparable results SPEC provides benchmarks for various systems. However, the one for Java, the SPECjvm98 [17], is usually too large for embedded systems.

Due to the absence of a *standard* Java benchmark for embedded systems, a small benchmark suit that should run on even the smallest device is provided here. It contains several micro-benchmarks for evaluating CPI for single bytecodes or short sequences of bytecodes, a synthetic benchmark (the Sieve of Eratosthenes) and two application benchmarks.

To provide a realistic workload for embedded systems, a real-time application was adapted to create the first application benchmark (Kfl). The application is taken from one of the nodes of a distributed motor control system [83] (see Section 7.5.1). A simulation of both the environment (sensors and actors) and the communication system (commands from the master station) forms part of the benchmark, so as to simulate the real-world workload. The second application benchmark is an adaptation of a tiny TCP/IP stack (Ejip) for embedded Java. This benchmark contains two UDP server/clients, exchanging messages via a loopback device.

As we will see, there is a great variation in processing power across different embedded systems. To cater for this variation, all benchmarks are 'self adjusting'. Each benchmark consists of an aspect that is benchmarked in a loop and an 'overhead' loop that contains any overheads from the benchmark that should be subtracted from the result (this feature is designed for the micro-benchmarks). The loop count adapts itself until the benchmark runs for more than a second. The number of iterations per second is then calculated, which means that higher values indicate better performance.

The benchmark framework only needs two system functions: one to measure time in millisecond resolution and one to print the results. These functions are encapsulated in LowLevel.java and can be adapted to environments, in which the full Java library is not available. For example, the leJOS system has very limited output capabilities and there is therefore a special LowLevel.java for this device. The following list gives a brief description of the Java systems that were benchmarked:

JOP is implemented in a Cyclone FPGA, running at 100MHz. The main memory is a 32-bit static RAM (15ns) with an access time of 3 clock cycles.

leJOS As an example for a low-end embedded device we use the RCX robot controller from the LEGO MindStorms series. It contains a 16-bit Hitachi H8300 microcontroller [41], running at 16MHz. leJOS [85] is a tiny interpreting JVM for the RCX.

TINI is an enhanced 8051 clone running a software JVM. The results were taken from a custom board with a 20MHz crystal, and the chip's PLL is set to a factor of 2. The TINIOS firmware revision running on the board is 1.12p9.

Komodo Komodo [55] is a Java processor as a basis for research on real-time scheduling on a multithreaded microcontroller (see Section 3.2.8). The benchmark results were obtained by Matthias Pfeffer [75] on a cycle-accurate simulation of Komodo. The values are obtained without garbage collection. According to Pfeffer, Komodo can be clocked with 33MHz in a Xlinix XCV800.

JStamp aJile's JEMCore is a direct-execution Java processor that is available in two different versions: the aJ-80 and the aJ-100 [2]. The aJ-100 provides a generic 8-bit, 16-bit or 32-bit external bus interface, while the aJ-80 only provides an 8-bit interface. A development system, the JStamp [91], was used for this benchmark. It contains the aJ-80, clocked at 74MHz.

SaJe is a board that contains the aJ-100 clocked with 100MHz and 10ns SRAM.

EJC The EJC (Embedded Java Controller) platform [27] is a typical example of a JIT system on a RISC processor. The system is based on a 32-bit ARM720T processor running at 74MHz. It contains up to 64 MB SDRAM and up to 16 MB of NOR flash.

SUN jvm is the Sun JVM 1.4.1, running on a 266MHz Pentium MMX under Linux.

gcj is the GNU compiler for Java. This configuration represents the batch compiler solution, running on a 266MHz Pentium.

Xint   As a reference the benchmark is also run with the Sun JVM in interpreting mode
(with option -Xint).

MB   is the realization of Java on a RISC processor for an FPGA (Xilinx MicroBlaze
[18]). Java is compiled to C with a Java compiler for real-time systems [72]
and the C program is compiled with the standard GNU toolchain.

In Figure 7.1, the geometric mean of the two application benchmarks is shown. The
unit used for the result is iterations per second. Note that the vertical axis is logarith-
mic, in order to obtain useful figures to show the great variation in performance. The
top diagram shows absolute performance, while the bottom diagram shows the same
results scaled to a 1MHz clock frequency. The results of the application benchmarks
and the geometric mean are shown in Table 7.4. The raw data for all benchmarks can
be found in Appendix E.

It should be noted that scaling to a single clock frequency could prove problematic.
The relation between processor clock frequency and memory access time cannot always be maintained. To give an example, if we were to increase the results of the
100MHz JOP to 1GHz, this would also involve reducing the memory access time
from 15ns to 1.5ns. Processors with 1GHz clock frequency are already available, but
the fastest asynchronous SRAM to date has an access time of 10ns.

To compare the performance relatively to the size of the different systems, Figure 7.2 shows the performance of JOP, the aJ100 and the two PC versions relative
to the gate count (from Table 7.3) and clock frequency. Relative to size and clock
frequency, JOP outperforms the aJile processor by a factor of 19 and even the JIT-
compiler on the Pentium MMX by a factor of 4.

All the benchmarks measure how often a function is executed per second. Therefore, execution time is only measured indirectly – a higher value means shorter execution time. In the Kfl benchmark, this function contains the main loop of the application (see Listing 7.2) that is executed in a periodic cycle in the original application.
In the benchmark the wait for the next period is omitted, so that the time measured
solely represents execution time. The UDP benchmark contains the generation of a
request, transmitting it through the UDP/IP stack, generating the answer and transmitting it back as a benchmark function. The iteration count is the number of received
answers per second.

In the application benchmarks, the main function is executed in a loop until one
second (or a longer period of time) has elapsed. For the application benchmark, there
is no 'overhead' loop. This feature is only used in the micro-benchmarks. As the
benchmark is self-adjusting, the measured time can also be longer than one second.
The result is the iteration count, scaled to one second.

	Frequency [MHz]	Kfl	UDP/IP	Geom. Mean [Iterations/s]	Per MHz
JOP	100	14,222	6,050	9,276	93
leJOS	16	25	13	18	1
TINI	40	64	29	43	1
Komodo	33	924	520	693	21
JStamp	74	2,221	1,004	1,493	20
SaJe	103	14,148	6,415	9,527	92
EJC	74	9,893	2,822	5,284	71
Sun jvm	266	212,952	91,851	139,857	526
gcj	266	139,884	38,460	73,348	276
Xint	266	17,310	8,747	12,305	46
MB 2KB/0KB	100	3,792			

Table 7.4: Application benchmarks on different Java systems. The table shows the benchmark results in iterations per second – a higher value means higher performance.

The accuracy of the measurement depends on the resolution of the system time. For the measurements under Linux, the system time has a resolution of 10ms, resulting in an inaccuracy of 1%. The accuracy of the system time on leJOS, TINI and the aJile is not known, but is considered to be in the same range. For JOP, a μs counter is used for time measurement.

Discussion

When comparing JOP and the aJile processor against leJOS and TINI, we can see that a Java processor is up to 500 times faster than an interpreting JVM on a standard processor for an embedded system. The average performance of JOP is a little bit better than a JIT-compiler solution on an embedded system, as represented by the EJC system.

Even when scaled to the same clock frequency, each compiling JVM on a PC (Sun jvm and gcj) is much faster than either embedded solution. However, as we saw in Section 5.8, the kernel of the application is smaller than 4KB. It therefore fits in the level one cache of the Pentium MMX (16KB + 16KB level one cache). For a comparison with a Pentium class processor we would need a larger application.

JOP is about 6 times faster than the aJ80 Java processor on the popular JStamp board. However, the aJ80 processor only contains an 8-bit memory interface, and

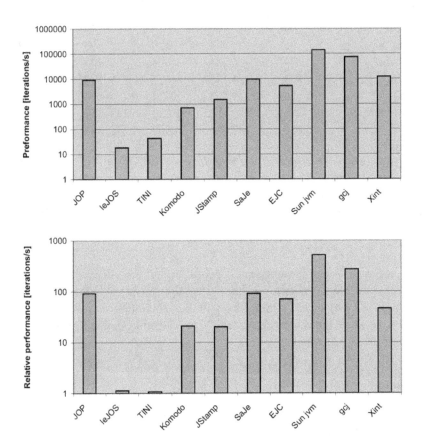

Figure 7.1: Performance comparison of different Java systems with application benchmarks. The diagrams show the geometric mean of the two benchmarks in iterations per second – a higher value means higher performance. The top diagram shows absolute performance, while the bottom diagram shows the result scaled to 1MHz clock frequency.

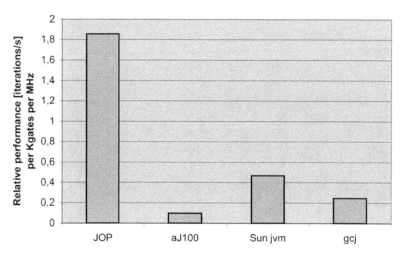

Figure 7.2: Performance comparison of different Java systems with application benchmarks. The diagram shows the result scaled to the chip size (Kgates) and clock frequency (MHz).

suffers from this bottleneck. The SaJe system contains the aJ100 with 32-bit, 10ns SRAMs and is as fast as JOP with its 15ns SRAMs.

The MicroBlaze system is a representation of a Java batch-compilation system for a RISC processor. MicroBlaze is configured with the same cache[4] as JOP and clocked at the same frequency. JOP is about three times faster than this solution, thus showing that native execution of Java bytecodes is faster than batch-compiled Java on a similar system. However, the results of the MicroBlaze solution are at a preliminary stage[5], as the Java2C compiler [72] is still under development.

The micro-benchmarks are intended to give insight into the implementation of the JVM. In Table 7.5, we can see the execution time in clock cycles of various byte-codes. As almost all bytecodes manipulate the stack, it is not possible to measure the execution time for a single bytecode. As a minimum requirement, a second instruction is necessary to reverse the stack operation.

For JOP we can deduce that the WCET for simple bytecodes (as given in Appendix D) is also the average execution time. We can see that the combination of iload and iadd executes in two cycles, which means that each of these two opera-

---

[4] The MicroBlaze with a 8KB data and 8KB instruction cache is about 2.5 times faster than JOP. However, a 16KB memory is not available in low-cost FPGAs and is an unbalanced system with respect to the LC/memory relation. Furthermore, the benchmark fits into a 4KB cache and the resulting measurement does not include main memory access.

[5] As not all language constructs can be compiled, only the Kfl benchmark was measured.

	JOP	leJOS	TINI	Komodo	JStamp	SaJe	Xint
iload iadd	2	836	789	8	38	8	17
iinc	11	422	388	4	41	11	2
ldc	10	1,340	1,128	40	67	9	31
if_icmplt taken	6	1,609	1,265	24	42	18	36
if_icmplt not taken	6	1,520	1,211	24	40	14	37
getfield	25	1,879	2,398	48	142	23	39
getstatic	17	1,676	4,463	80	102	15	40
iaload	30	1,082	1,543	28	74	13	30
invoke	128	4,759	6,495	384	349	112	182
invoke static	101	3,875	5,869	680	271	92	164
invoke interface	146	5,094	6,797	1617	531	148	193

Table 7.5: Execution time in clock cycles for various JVM bytecodes

tions is executed in a single cycle. The iinc bytecode is one of the few instructions that do not manipulate the stack and can be measured alone. As iinc is not implemented in hardware, we have a total of 11 cycles that are executed in microcode. It is fair to assume that this comprises too great an overhead for an instruction that is found in every iterative loop with an integer index. However, the decision to implement this instruction in microcode was derived from the observation that the dynamic instruction count for iinc is only 2% (see Section 5.1).

The sequence for the branch benchmark (if_icmplt) contains the two load instructions that push the arguments onto the stack. The arguments are then consumed by the branch instruction. This benchmark verifies that a branch requires a constant four cycles on JOP, whether it is taken or not.

For compiling versions of the JVM, these micro-benchmarks do not produce useful results. The compiler performs optimizations that make it impossible to measure execution times at this fine a granularity.

During the evaluation of the aJile system, unexpected behavior was observed. The aJ80 on the JStamp board is clocked at 7.3728MHz and the internal frequency can be set with a PLL. The aJ80 is rated for 80MHz and the maximum PLL factor that can be used is therefore ten. Running the benchmarks with different PLL settings gave some strange results. For example, with a PLL multiplier setting of ten, the aJ80 was about 12.8 times faster! Other PLL factors also resulted in a greater than linear speedup. The only explanation we could find was that the internal time, System.currentTimeMillis(), used for the benchmarks depends on the PLL setting. A comparison with the wall clock time showed that the internal time of the aJ80 is 23% faster with a PLL factor of 1 and 2.4% faster with a factor of ten – a property we would not expect on a processor that is marketed for real-time systems.

The SaJe board is also clocked with 7.3728MHz and the PLL factor is set to 14. This gives a 103.2192MHz internal clock frequency. However, it is not known how accurate the internal time is in this setting. The results for the SaJe board can also suffer from the problem described above.

Execution Time Jitter

For real-time systems, the worst-case of the execution time is of primary importance. We have measured the execution times of several iterations of the main function from the Kfl benchmark. Figure 7.3 shows the measurements, scaled to the minimum execution time.

A period of four iterations can be seen. This period results from simulating the commands from the base station that are executed every fourth iteration. At iteration 10, a command to start the motor is issued. We see the resulting rise in execution time at iteration 12 to process this command. At iteration 54, the simulation triggers the end sensor and the motor is stopped.

The different execution times in the different modes of the application are inherent in the design of the simulation. However, the ratio between the longest and the shortest period is five for the JStamp, four for the gcj system and only three for JOP. Therefore, a system with an aJile processor needs to be 1.7 times faster than JOP in order to provide the same WCET for this measurement. At iteration 33, we can see a higher execution time for the JStamp system that is not seen on JOP. This variation at iteration 33 is not caused by the benchmark.

The execution time under gcj on the Linux system showed some very high peaks (up to ten times the minimum, not shown in the figures). This observation was to be expected, as the gcj/Linux system is not a real-time solution. The Sun JIT-solution is omitted from the figure. As a result of the invocation of the compiler at some point during the simulation, the worst-case ratio between the maximum and minimum execution time was 1313 – showing that a JIT-compiler is impractical for real-time applications.

It should be noted that execution time measurement is not a safe method for obtaining WCET estimates. However, in situations where no WCET analysis tool is available, it can give some insight into the WCET behavior of different systems.

7.3.2 Real-Time Performance

In this section, the implementation of the simple real-time profile (from Section 6.1) with JOP is compared with the Reference Implementation (RI) of the RTSJ (see Sec-

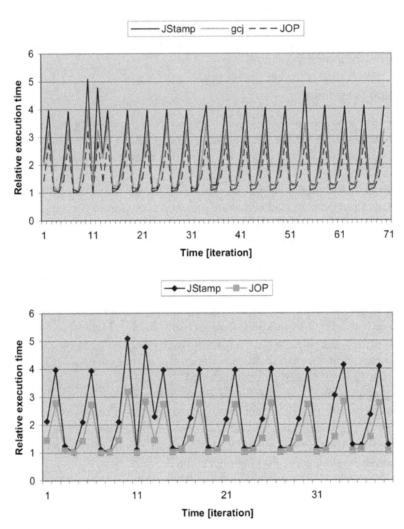

Figure 7.3: Execution time of the main function for the Kfl benchmark. The values are scaled to the minimum execution time. The bottom figure shows a detail of the top figure.

Period [μs]	Avg. [μs]	Std. Dev. [μs]	Min. [μs]	Max. [μs]
50	50	13	35	63
70	70	0	70	70
100	100	0	100	100
500	500	0	500	500
1,000	1,000	0	1,000	1,000

Table 7.6: Jitter of periodic threads with JOP

tion 4.4.3) on top of Linux. We use the Linux platform for the comparison, as it is the only platform for which the RTSJ is available. The RI is an interpreting implementation of the JVM that is, however, not optimized for performance. A commercial version of the RTSJ, JTime by TimeSys, should perform better. However, it was not possible to get a license of JTime for research purposes. JOP is implemented in Altera's low-cost Cyclone EP1C6 FPGA, and clocked with 100MHz. The test results for the RI were obtained on an Intel Pentium MMX 266MHz, running Linux with two different kernels: a generic kernel version 2.4.20 and the real-time kernel from TimeSys [92], as recommended for the RI. For each test, 500 measurements were taken. Time was measured using a hardware counter in JOP and the time stamp counter of the Pentium processor under Linux.

Periodic Threads

Many activities in real-time systems must be performed periodically. Low release jitter is of major importance for tasks such as control loops. The test setting is similar to the periodic thread test in [20]. A single real-time thread only calls waitForNextPeriod() in a loop and records the time between subsequent calls. A second idle thread, with a lower priority, merely consumes processing time. This test setting results in two context switches per period. Table 7.6 shows the average, standard deviation and extreme values for different period times on JOP. The same values are shown in Table 7.7 for the RI. Please note that the values are in μs for JOP and in ms for the RI.

Using microsecond accurate timer interrupts, programmed by the scheduler, results in excellent performance of periodic threads in JOP. No jitter from the scheduler can be seen with a single thread at periods longer than $70\mu s$.

The measurement for the RI excludes the first values measured. The first values are misleading as the RI behaves unpredictably at *startup*. The RI performs inaccurately

Period [ms]	Avg. [ms]	Std. Dev. [ms]	Min. [ms]	Max. [ms]
5	4.0	7.92	0.017	19.90
10	6.6	9.34	0.019	19.94
20	20.0	0.015	19.87	20.14
35	35.0	5.001	29.75	40.25
50	50.0	0.018	49.95	50.06
100	100.0	0.002	99.94	100.1

Table 7.7: Jitter of periodic threads with RI/RTSJ

	Avg.	Std. Dev.	Min.	Max.
JOP	2,686	14	2,676	2,709
RI Linux	4,253	1,239	3,232	19,628
RI TS Linux	12,923	1,145	11,529	21,090

Table 7.8: Time for a thread switch in clock cycles

at periods below 20ms. This effect has also been observed in [19]. Larger periods that are multiples of 10ms have very low jitter. However, using a period such as 35ms shows a standard deviation of five ms. A detailed look into the collected samples only shows values of 30 and 40ms. This implies a timer tick of 10ms in the underlying operating system. No significant difference is observed when running this test on the generic Linux kernel and the TimeSys kernel. The commercial version of the TimeSys Linux kernel should perform better as the resolution of the timer tick is 1ms and a programmable time can be used for periodic threads. However, it was not possible to obtain a license to evaluate the combination of JTime on the commercial Linux kernel. Table 7.7 represents the measurements on the generic kernel. This comparison shows the advantage of an adjustable timer interrupt over a fixed timer tick.

Context Switch

This test setting consists of two threads. A low priority thread continuously stores the current time in a shared variable. A high priority periodic thread measures the time difference between this value and the time immediately after `waitForNextPeriod()`. Table 7.8 gives the times for the context switch in processor clock cycles.

	Avg.	Std. Dev.	Min.	Max.
JOP	2,935	7	2,773	2,935
RI Linux	53,685	7,014	47,400	87,196
RI TS Linux	69,273	7,832	63,060	101,292

Table 7.9: Dispatch latency of event handlers in clock cycles

This test did not produce the expected behavior from the RI on the generic Linux kernel. When the low priority thread ran in this tight loop, the high priority thread was not scheduled. After inserting a Thread.yield() and an operating system call, such as System.out.print(), in this loop, the test performed as expected. This indicates a major problem in either the RI or the operating system scheduler. This problem did not occur when the RI was run on the TimeSys Linux kernel. However, the context switch time on the TimeSys kernel is three times longer than on the standard kernel.

Asynchronous Event Handler

In this test setting, a high priority event handler is triggered by a low priority periodic thread. As AsynchEventHandler performs poorly in the RI (see [19]), a BoundAsynchEventHandler is used for the RI test program. The time elapsed between the invocation of fire() and the first statement of the event handler was measured. Table 7.9 shows the elapsed times in clock cycles for JOP and the RTSJ RI.

The time taken to dispatch an asynchronous event is similar to the context switch time in JOP. This is to be expected as events are scheduled and dispatched as threads. The minimum value only occurred in the first event, all following events having been dispatched in the maximum time.

In the RI, the dispatch time is about 12 times larger than a context switch with a significant variation in time. This indicates that the implementation of fire() and the communication of the event to the underlying operating system are not optimal. The time factor between context switch and event handling on the TimeSys kernel is lower than on the standard kernel, but is nevertheless still significant.

Summary

In this section, we have compared the RTSJ on top of Linux with the implementation of a simple real-time profile on top of JOP. The RTSJ addresses several issues relating to the use of Java for real-time systems. However, the RTSJ is a specification too large and complex to be implemented in small embedded systems. We therefore use the simpler real-time profile for JOP. Tight integration of the real-time scheduler with the supporting processor results in an efficient platform for Java in embedded real-time systems. A performance comparison between this implementation and the RTSJ showed that a dedicated Java processor without an underlying operating system is more predictable than trying to adopt a general purpose OS for real-time systems. Time will show if an implementation of the RTSJ on a *real* RTOS will outperform the presented solution.

7.4 WCET

Worst-case execution time (WCET) estimates of tasks are essential for designing and verifying real-time systems. WCET estimates can be obtained either by measurement or static analysis. The problem with using measurements is that the execution times of tasks tend to be sensitive to their inputs. As a rule, measurement does not guarantee safe WCET estimates. Instead, static analysis is necessary for hard real-time systems. Static analysis is usually divided into a number of different phases:

Path analysis generates the control flow graph (a directed graph of basic blocks) of the program and annotates (manual or automatic) loops with bounds.

Low-level analysis determines the execution time of basic blocks obtained by the path analysis. A model of the processor and the pipeline provides the execution time for the instruction sequence.

Global low-level analysis determines the influence of hardware features such as caches on program execution time. This analysis can use information from the path analysis to provide less pessimistic values.

WCET Calculation collapses the control flow graph to provide the final WCET estimate. Alternative paths in the graph are collapsed to a single value (the largest of the alternatives) and loops are collapsed once the loop bound is known.

For the low-level analysis, a good timing model of the processor is needed. The main problem for the low-level analysis is the execution time dependency of instructions in modern processors that are not designed for real-time systems. JOP is designed to be an easy target for WCET analysis. The WCET of each bytecode can be predicted in terms of number of cycles it requires. There are no dependencies between bytecodes.

Each bytecode is implemented by microcode. We can obtain the WCET of a single bytecode by performing WCET analysis at the microcode level. To prove that there are no time dependencies between bytecodes, we have to show that no processor states are *shared* between different bytecodes.

7.4.1 Microcode Path Analysis

To obtain the WCET values for the individual bytecodes we perform the path analysis at the microcode level. First, we have to ensure that a number of restrictions (from [78]) of the code are fulfilled:

- Programs must not contain unbounded recursion. This property is satisfied by the fact that there exists no call instruction in microcode.

- Function pointers and computed gotos complicate the path analysis and should therefore be avoided. Only simple conditional branches are available at the microcode level.

- The upper bound of each loop has to be known. This is the only point that has to be verified by inspection of the microcode.

To detect loops in the microcode we have to find all backward branches (e.g. with a negative branch offset). The branch offsets can be found in a VHDL file (offtbl.vhd) that is generated during microcode assembly. In the current implementation of the JVM there are ten different negative offsets. However, not each offset represents a loop. Most of these branches are used to share common code. All backward branches found in jvm.asm are summarized below:

- Three branches are found in the initialization code of the JVM. They are not part of a bytecode implementation and can be ignored.

- Five branches are used by exceptions, the interrupt bytecode, and for the call of Java implemented bytecodes. The target of these branches is found in the implementation of invoke to share part of the microcode sequence. These branches are therefore not part of a loop.

- One branch is found in the implementation of imul to perform a fixed delay. The iteration count for this loop is constant.

- Two backward branches share the same offset and are used in loops to move data between the stack memory and main memory. This loop is not part of a regular bytecode. It is contained in a system function used by the scheduler for the task switch. The bound for this loop has to be determined in the scheduler code.

A few bytecodes are implemented in Java. The implementation can be found in the class com.jopdesign.sys.JVM and can be analyzed in the same way as application code. The bytecodes idiv and irem contain a constant loop. The bytecodes new and `anewarray` contain loops to initialize (with zero values) new objects or arrays. The loop is bound by the size of the object or array. The bytecode `lookupswitch`[6] performs a linear search through a table of branch offsets. The WCET depends on the table size that can be found as part of the instruction.

As the microcode sequences are very short, the calculation of the control flow graph for each bytecode is done manually.

7.4.2 Microcode Low-level Analysis

To calculate the execution time of basic blocks in the microcode, we need to establish the timing of microcode instructions on JOP. All microcode instructions except `wait` execute in a single cycle, reducing the low-level analysis to a case of merely counting the instructions.

The `wait` instruction is used to stall the processor and wait for the memory subsystem to finish a memory transaction. The execution time of the `wait` instruction depends on the memory system and, if the memory system is predictable, has a known WCET. A main memory consisting of SRAM chips can provide this predictability and this solution is therefore advised. The predictable handling of DMA, which is used for the instruction cache fill, is explained in Section 5.8.3. The `wait` instruction is the only way to stall the processor. Hardware events, such as interrupts (see Section 5.4.5), do not stall the processor.

Microcode is stored in on-chip memory with single cycle access. Each microcode instruction is a single word long and there is no need for either caching or prefetching at this stage. We can therefore omit performing a low-level analysis. No pipeline analysis [28], with its possible unbound timing effects, is necessary.

7.4.3 Bytecode Independency

We have seen that all microcode instructions except `wait` take one cycle to execute and are therefore independent of other instructions. This property directly translates to independency of bytecode instructions.

The `wait` microcode instruction provides a convenient way to hide memory access time. A memory read or write can be triggered in microcode (with `stmra` and `stmwd`) and the processor can continue with microcode instructions. When the data from a memory read is needed, the processor explicitly waits until it becomes available.

For a memory store, this wait can be deferred until the memory system is used next. It is possible to initiate the store in a bytecode such as `putfield` and continue

---

[6]`lookupswitch` is one way of implementing the Java switch statement. The other bytecode, `tableswitch`, uses an index in the table of branch offsets and has therefore a constant execution time.

with the execution of the next bytecode, even when the store has not been completed. In this case, we introduce a dependency over bytecode boundaries, as the state of the memory system is *shared*. To avoid these dependencies that are difficult to analyze, each bytecode that accesses memory waits (preferably at the end of the microcode sequence) for the memory system.

Furthermore, the deferring of wait in a store operation results in an additional wait in every read operation. Since read operations are more frequent than write operations (15% vs. 2.5%, see Section 5.1), the performance gain from the hidden memory store is lost.

7.4.4 WCET of Bytecodes

The control flow of the individual bytecodes together with the basic block length (that directly corresponds with the execution time) and the time for memory access result in the WCET (and BCET) values of the bytecodes. These values can be found in Appendix D.

7.4.5 Evaluation

We conclude this section with a worst and best case analysis of a classic example, the Bubble Sort algorithm. The values calculated are compared with the measurements of the execution time on JOP on all permutations of the input data. Figure 7.1 shows the test program in Java. The algorithm contains two nested loops and one condition. We use an array of five elements to perform the measurements for all permutations (i.e. $5! = 120$) of the input data. The number of iterations of the outer loop is one less than the array size: $c_1 = N - 1$, in this case four. The inner loop is executed $c_2 = \sum_{i=1}^{c_1} i = c_1(c_1 + 1)/2$ times, i.e. ten times in our example.

The compiled version, i.e. the bytecodes of the test program, split into basic blocks, is given in Table 7.10. The fourth column contains the execution time of the byte-codes and the basic blocks in clock cycles.

The annotated control flow graph (CFG) of the example is shown in Figure 7.4. The edges contain labels showing how often the path between two nodes is taken. We can identify the outer loop, containing the blocks B2, B3, B4 and B8. The inner loop consists of blocks B4, B5, B6 and B7. Block B6 is executed when the condition of the if statement is true. The path from B5 to B7 is the only path that depends on the input data.

```java
final static int N = 5;

static void sort(int[] a) {

    int i, j, v1, v2;
    // loop count = N–1
    for (i=N–1; i>0; —i) {
        // loop count = (N–1)*N/2
        for (j=1; j<=i; ++j) {
            v1 = a[j–1];
            v2 = a[j];
            if (v1 > v2) {
                a[j] = v1;
                a[j–1] = v2;
            }
        }
    }
}
```

Listing 7.1: Bubble Sort in Java

Block	Addr.	Bytecode	Cycles	WCET Count	WCET Total	BCET Count	BCET Total
B1			2	1	2	1	2
	0:	iconst_4	1				
	1:	istore_1	1				
B2			5	5	25	5	25
	2:	iload_1	1				
	3:	ifle 53	4				
B3			2	4	8	4	8
	6:	iconst_1	1				
	7:	istore_2	1				
B4			6	14	84	14	84
	8:	iload_2	1				
	9:	iload_1	1				
	10:	if_icmpgt 47	4				
B5			74	10	740	10	740
	13:	aload_0	1				
	14:	iload_2	1				
	15:	iconst_1	1				
	16:	isub	1				
	17:	iaload	29				
	18:	istore_3	1				
	19:	aload_0	1				
	20:	iload_2	1				
	21:	iaload	29				
	22:	istore 4	2				
	24:	iload_3	1				
	25:	iload 4	2				
	27:	if_icmple 41	4				
B6			73	10	730	0	0
	30:	aload_0	1				
	31:	iload_2	1				
	32:	iload_3	1				
	33:	iastore	32				
	34:	aload_0	1				
	35:	iload_2	1				
	36:	iconst_1	1				

Table 7.10: WCET and BCET in clock cycles of the Bubble Sort test program

Block	Addr.	Bytecode	Cycles	WCET Count	WCET Total	BCET Count	BCET Total
	37:	isub	1				
	38:	iload 4	2				
	40:	iastore	32				
B7			15	10	150	10	150
	41:	iinc 2, 1	11				
	44:	goto 8	4				
B8			15	4	60	4	60
	47:	iinc 1, -1	11				
	50:	goto 2	4				
B9				1		1	
	53:	return					
Execution time calculated					1,799		1,069
Execution time measured					1,799		1,069

Table 7.10: WCET and BCET in clock cycles of the Bubble Sort test program

The values in the fifth and seventh columns (Count) of Table 7.10 are derived from the CFG and show how often the basic blocks are executed in the worst and best cases. The WCET and BCET value for each block is calculated by multiplying the clock cycles by the execution frequency. The overall WCET and BCET values are calculated by summing the values of the individual blocks B1 to B8. The last block (B9) is omitted, as the measurement does not contain the return statement.

The execution time of the program is measured using the cycle counter in JOP. The current time is taken at both the entry of the method and at the end, resulting in a measurement spanning from block B1 to the beginning of block B9. The last statement, the `return`, is not part of the measurement. The difference between these two values (less the additional 8 cycles introduced by the measurement itself) is given as the execution time in clock cycles (the last row in Table 7.10). The measured WCET and BCET values are exactly the same as the calculated values.

In Figure 7.5, the measured execution times for all 120 permutations of the input data are shown. The vertical axis shows the execution time in clock cycles and the horizontal axis the number of the test run. The first input sample is an already sorted array and results in the lowest execution time. The last sample is the worst-case value resulting from the reversely ordered input data. We can also see the 11 different execution times that result from executing basic block B6 (which performs the element exchange and takes 73 clock cycles) between 0 and 10 times.

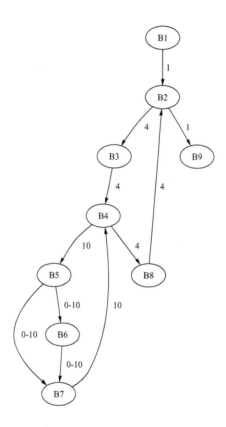

Figure 7.4: The control flow graph of the Bubble Sort example

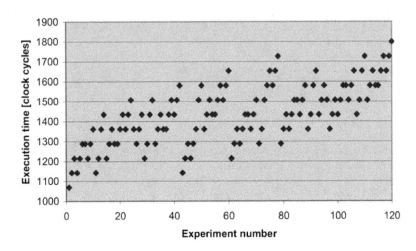

Figure 7.5: Execution time in clock cycles of the Bubble Sort program

This example has demonstrated that JOP is a simple target for the WCET analysis. Most bytecodes have a single execution time (WCET = BCET), and the WCET of a task depends only on the control flow. No pipeline or data dependencies complicate the low-level part of the WCET analysis.

7.5 Applications

During the research for this thesis, the first working version of JOP was used in a real-world application. Using an architecture under development in a commercial project entails risks. Nevertheless, this was deemed to be the best way to prove the feasibility of the processor. In this section, the experiences of the first project involving JOP are summarized.

7.5.1 Motor Control

In rail cargo, a large amount of time is spent on loading and unloading of goods wagons. The contact wire above the wagons is the main obstacle. Balfour Beatty Austria developed and patented a technical solution, the so-called *Kippfahrleitung*, to tilt up the contact wire. This is done on a line up to one kilometer. An asynchrony motor on each mast is used for this tilting. However, it has to be done synchronously on the whole line.

Each motor is controlled by an embedded system. This system also measures the

Figure 7.6: Picture of a *Kippfahrleitung* mast in down and up position

position and communicates with a base station. Figure 7.6 shows the mast with the motor and the control system in the 'down' and 'up' positions. The base station has to control the deviation of individual positions during the tilt. It also includes the user interface for the operator. In technical terms, this is a distributed, embedded real-time control system, communicating over an RS485 network.

Real Hardware

Although this system is not mass-produced, there were nevertheless cost constraints. Even a small FPGA is more expensive than a general purpose CPU. To compensate for this, additional chips for the memory and the FPGA configuration were optimized for cost. One standard 128KB Flash was used to hold FPGA configuration data, the Java program and a logbook. External main memory was reduced to 128KB with an 8-bit data bus.

To reduce external components, the boot process is a little complicated. A watchdog circuit delivers a reset signal to a 32 macro-cell PLD. This PLD loads the configuration data into the FPGA. When the FPGA starts, it disables the PLD and loads the Java program from the Flash into the external RAM. After the JVM is initialized, the program starts at main().

The motor is controlled by silicon switches connected to the FPGA with opto couplers. The position is measured with two end sensors and a revolving sensor. The processor supervises the voltage and current of the motor supply. A display and keyboard are attached to the base station for user interface. The communication bus (up to one kilometer) is attached via an isolated RS485 data interface.

Synthesized Hardware

The following I/O modules were added to the JOP core in the FPGA:

- Timer

- UART for debugging

- UART with FIFO for the RS485 line

- Four sigma delta ADCs

- I/O ports

Five switches in the power line needed to be controlled by the program. A wrong setting of the switches due to a software error could result in a short circuit. Ensuring that this could not happen was a straightforward task at the VHDL level. The sigma-delta ADCs are used to measure the temperature of the silicon switches and the current through the motor.

Software Architecture

The main task of the program was to measure the position using the revolving sensor and communicate with the base station. This has to be done under real-time constraints. This is not a very complicated task. However, at the time of development, many features from a full-blown JVM implementation, such as threads or objects, were missing in JOP. The resulting Java was more like a *tiny Java*. It had to be kept in mind which Java constructs were supported by JOP. Because there was no multithreading capability, and in the interests of simplicity, a simple infinite loop with constant time intervals was used. Listing 7.2 shows the simplified program structure. After initialization and memory allocation, this loop was entered and did never exit.

Communication

Communication is based on a client server structure. Only the base station is allowed to send a request to a single mast station. This station is then required to reply. The maximum reply time is bounded by two time intervals. The base station handles

```java
public static void main(String[] args) {

    init();
    Timer.start();
    forever();
    // this point is NEVER reached
}

private static void forever() {

    for (;;) {
        Msg.loop();
        Triac.loop();
        if (Msg.available) {
            handleMsg();
        } else {
            chkMsgTimeout();
        }
        handleWatchDog();
        Timer.waitForNextInterval();
    }
}
```

Listing 7.2: Simplified program structure

timeout and retry. If an irrecoverable error occurs, the base station switches off the power to the mast stations, including the power supply to the motor. This is the safe state of the whole system.

From the mast station perspective, every mast station supervises the base station. The base station is required to send requests on a regular basis. If this requirement is violated, the mast station switches off its motor. The data is exchanged in small packets of four bytes, including a one-byte CRC. To simplify the development, commands to program the Flash in the mast stations and force a reset were included. It is therefore possible to update the program, or even change the FPGA configuration, over the network.

7.5.2 Further Projects

TAL, short for TeleAlarm, is a remote tele-control and data logging system. TAL communicates via a modem or an Ethernet bus with a SCADA system or via SMS with a mobile phone. For this application, a minimal TCP/IP stack needed to be implemented. This stack was the reason for implementing threads and a simple real-time system in JOP.

Another application of JOP is in a communication device with soft real-time properties – Austrian Railways' (ÖBB) new security system for single-track lines. Each locomotive is equipped with a GPS receiver and a communication device. The position of the train, differential correction data for GPS and commands are exchanged with a server at the central station over a GPRS virtual private network. JOP is the heart of the communication device in the locomotive. The flexibility of the FPGA and an Internet connection to the embedded system make it possible to upgrade the software and even the processor in the field.

7.6 Summary

In this chapter, we presented an evaluation of JOP. We have seen that JOP is the smallest hardware realization of the JVM available to date. Due to the efficient implementation of the stack architecture, JOP is also smaller than a *comparable* RISC processor in an FPGA. Implemented in an FPGA, JOP has the highest clock frequency of all known Java processors.

We compared JOP against several embedded Java systems and, as a reference, with Java on a standard PC. A Java processor is up to 500 times faster than an interpreting JVM on a standard processor for an embedded system. JOP is about six times faster than the aJ80 Java processor and as fast as the aJ100[7]. Preliminary results using compiled Java for a RISC processor in an FPGA, with a similar resource usage and maximum clock frequency to JOP, showed that native execution of Java bytecodes is faster than compiled Java.

We compared the basic properties of the real-time scheduler on JOP against the RTSJ implementation on Linux. The integration of the scheduler in the JVM, and the timer interrupt under scheduler control, results in an efficient platform for Java in embedded real-time systems. JOP performs better and more predictably than the reference implementation of the RTSJ under Linux.

We also performed WCET analysis of the implemented JVM at the microcode level. This analysis provides the WCET and BCET values for the individual bytecodes. We have also shown that there are no dependencies between individual bytecodes. This feature, in combination with the method cache (see Section 5.8), makes JOP an easy target for low-level WCET analysis of Java applications.

Usage of JOP in three real-world applications showed that the processor is mature enough to be used in commercial projects.

---

[7]The measured aJ100 system contained faster SRAMs than the FPGA board for JOP.

8 Conclusions

In this chapter we will undertake a short review of the thesis and summarize the contributions. Java for real-time systems is a very new and active research area. This chapter is completed by suggestions for future research, based on the proposed Java processor.

8.1 Conclusions

In the following list, we draw conclusions about the Java processor presented in this thesis, in relation to the problem stated in Section 3.4:

1. A time-predictable Java platform has been demonstrated. As shown in Section 5.7 and 5.8, the architectural design decisions and a time-predictable cache provide the basis for a time-predictable Java processor. In Section 7.4, it was shown that all bytecodes have a known WCET and there are no pipeline dependencies. JOP's architecture can therefore be modeled cycle-accurately for the low-level WCET analysis.

2. The implementation of a RISC-style stack architecture, with a novel mapping of Java bytecodes to microcode addresses (see Section 5.3), and the analysis of the JVM stack usage pattern (see Section 5.5) with the resource-efficient two-level stack cache resulted in a small design. In fact, JOP is the smallest implementation of the JVM in hardware available to date.

3. The usage of JOP in real-world applications, as described in Section 7.5, shows that JOP is a working processor and not only a theoretical architecture.

4. Comparing JOP with various embedded Java solutions in Section 7.3 showed that the time-predictable processor architecture does not need to be slow. JOP's average performance is similar to that of non real-time Java systems.

5. The flexibility of an FPGA allows for a HW/SW-co-design approach, with the aim of generating application-specific configurations of JOP.

6. In Section 6.1, a simple real-time profile for Java was defined. This profile solves a number of issues that arise from using standard Java for real-time systems. This profile was elaborated upon in Section 6.2 to create a framework for a user-defined scheduler in Java, thus enabling the implementation of advanced scheduling concepts at the application level.

8.2 Summary of Contributions

The research contributions made by this thesis are related to two areas: real-time Java and resource-constrained embedded systems.

A Real-Time Java Processor

The goal of time-predictable execution of Java programs was a first-class guiding principle throughout the development of JOP:

- The execution time for Java bytecodes can be exactly predicted in terms of the number of clock cycles. JOP is therefore a straightforward target for low-level WCET analysis. There is no mutual dependency between consecutive bytecodes that could result in unbounded timing effects.

- In order to provide time-predictable execution of Java bytecodes, the processor pipeline is designed without any prefetching or queuing. This fact avoids hard-to-analyze and possibly unbounded pipeline dependencies. There are no pipeline stalls, caused by interrupts or the memory subsystem, to complicate the WCET analysis.

- A pipelined processor architecture calls for higher memory bandwidth. A standard technique to avoid processing bottlenecks due to the higher memory bandwidth is caching. However, standard cache organizations improve the average execution time but are difficult to predict for WCET analysis. Two time-predictable caches are proposed for JOP: a *stack cache* as a substitution for the data cache and a *method cache* to cache the instructions.

  As the stack is a heavily accessed memory region, the stack – or part of it – is placed in local memory. This part of the stack is referred to as the *stack cache* and described in Section 5.5. Fill and spill of the stack cache is subjected to microcode control and therefore time-predictable.

  In Section 5.8, a novel way to organize an instruction cache, as *method cache*, is given. The cache stores complete methods, and cache misses only occur on method invocation and return. Cache block replacement depends on the call tree, instead of instruction addresses. This *method cache* is easy to analyze with respect to worst-case behavior and still provides substantial performance gain when compared against a solution without an instruction cache.

- The above described time-predictable processor provides the basis for real-time Java. The issues with standard Java and the Real-Time Specification for Java were analyzed in Chapter 4. To enable real-time Java to operate on resource-constrained devices, a simple real-time profile was defined in Section 6.1 and implemented in Java on JOP. The beauty of this approach is in implementing functions usually associated with an RTOS in Java. This means that real-time Java is not based on an RTOS, and therefore not restricted to the functionality provided by the RTOS. With JOP, a self-contained real-time system in pure Java becomes possible.

  The tight integration of the scheduler and the hardware that generates schedule events results in low latency and low jitter of the task dispatch.

- The defined real-time profile suggests a new way to handle hardware interrupts to avoid interference between blocking device drivers and application tasks. Hardware interrupts other than the timer interrupt are represented as asynchronous events with an associated thread. These events are *normal* schedulable objects and subject to the control of the scheduler. With a minimum interarrival time, these events, and the associated device drivers, can be incorporated into the priority assignment and schedulability analysis in the same way as normal application tasks.

The above-described contributions result in a time-predictable execution environment for real-time applications written in Java, without the resource implications and unpredictability of a JIT-compiler. The proposed processor architecture is a straightforward target for low-level WCET analysis.

Implementing a real-time scheduler in Java opens up new possibilities. The scheduler is extended to provide a framework for user-defined scheduling in Java. In Section 6.2, we analyzed which events are exposed to the scheduler and which functions from the JVM need to be available in the user space. A simple-to-use framework to evaluate new scheduling concepts is given.

A Resource-Constrained Processor

Embedded systems are usually very resource-constrained. Using a low-cost FPGA as the main target technology forced the design to be small. The following architectural features address this issue:

- The architecture of JOP is best described as:

    The JVM is a CISC stack architecture, whereas JOP is a RISC stack
    architecture.

    JOP contains its own instruction set, called microcode in this thesis, with a
    novel way of mapping bytecodes to microcode addresses. This mapping has
    zero overheads as described in Section 5.3. Basic bytecode instructions have a
    one-to-one mapping to microcode instructions and therefore execute in a single
    cycle. The stack architecture allows compact encoding of microinstructions in
    8 bit to save internal memory.

    This approach allows flexible implementation of Java bytecodes in hardware,
    as a microcode sequence or even in Java itself.

- The analysis of the JVM stack usage pattern in Section 5.5 led to the design
  of a resource-efficient two-level stack cache. This two-level stack cache fits to
  the embedded memory technologies of current FPGAs and ASICs and ensures
  fast execution of basic instructions.

    Part of the stack cache, which is implemented in an on-chip memory, is also
    used for microcode variables and constants. This resource sharing does not
    only reduce the number of memory blocks needed for the processor, but also
    the number of data paths to and from the execution unit.

- Interrupts are considered hard to handle in a pipelined processor, resulting in
  a complex (and therefore resource consuming) implementation. In JOP, the
  above mentioned bytecode-microcode mapping is used in a clever way to avoid
  interrupt handling in the core pipeline. Interrupts generate special bytecodes
  that are inserted in a transparent way in the bytecode stream. Interrupt handlers can be implemented in the same way as bytecodes are implemented: in
  microcode or in Java.

The above design decisions where chosen to keep the size of the processor small
without sacrificing performance. JOP is the smallest Java processor available to date
that provides the basis for an implementation of the CLDC specification (see Section 4.3.1). JOP is a fast execution environment for Java, without the resource implications and unpredictability of a JIT-compiler. The average performance of JOP is
similar to that of mainstream, non real-time Java systems.

JOP is a flexible architecture that allows different configurations for different application domains. Therefore, size can be traded against performance. As an example,

resource intensive instructions, such as floating point operations, can be implemented in Java. The flexibility of an FPGA implementation also allows adding application-specific hardware accelerators to JOP.

The small size of the processor allows usage of low-cost FPGAs in embedded systems that can compete against standard microcontroller. JOP has been implemented in several different FPGA families and is used in different real-world applications.

Programs for embedded and real-time systems are usually multi-threaded and a small design provides a path to a multi-processor system in a mid-sized FPGA or in an ASIC.

A tiny architecture also opens new application fields when implemented in an ASIC. Smart sensors and actuators, for example, are very sensitive to cost, which is proportional to the die area.

8.3 Future Research Directions

JOP provides a basis for various directions for future research. Some suggestions are given below:

Real-time garbage collector: In Section 6.1, a real-time profile was defined that avoids the unpredictability of a garbage collector. However, there have been advances in the research field of real-time GCs. Hardware support of a real-time GC would be an interesting topic for further research.

Another question that remains with a real-time GC is the analysis of the worst-case memory consumptions of tasks (similar to the WCET values), and scheduling the GC so that it can keep up with the allocation rate.

Hardware accelerator: The flexibility of an FPGA implementation of a processor opens up new possibilities for hardware accelerators. We have shown in Section 5.6 how the implementation of a bytecode can be moved between hardware and software. A further step would be to generate an application specific-system in which part of the application code is moved to hardware. Ideally, the hardware description should be extracted automatically from the Java source. Preliminary work in this area, using JOP as its basis, can be found in [35].

Hardware scheduler: In JOP, scheduling and dispatch is done in Java (with some microcode support). For tasks with very short periods, the scheduling overheads can prove to be too high. A scheduler implemented in hardware can shorten this time, due to the parallel nature of the algorithm.

Multiprocessor JVM: In order to generate a small and predictable processor, several advanced and resource-consuming features (such as instruction folding or branch prediction) were omitted from the design. The resulting low resource usage of JOP makes it possible to integrate more than one processor in an FPGA. Since embedded applications are naturally multi-threaded systems, the performance can easily be enhanced using a multi-processor solution. A multi-processor JVM with shared memory offers following research possibilities: scheduling of Java threads and synchronization between the processors; WCET analysis for the shared memory access.

Instruction cache: The cache solution proposed in Section 5.8 provides predictable instruction cache behavior while, in the average case, still performing in a similar way to a direct-mapped cache. However, an analysis tool for the worst-case behavior is still needed. With this tool, and a more complex analysis tool for traditional instruction caches, we also need to verify that the worst-case miss penalty is lower than with a traditional instruction cache.

A second interesting aspect of the proposed method cache is the fact that the replacement decision on a cache miss only occurs on method invoke and return. The infrequency of this decision means that more time is available for more advanced replacement algorithms.

Real-time Java: Although there is already a definition for real-time Java, i.e. the RTSJ [8], this definition is not necessarily adequate. There is ongoing research on how memory should be managed for real-time Java applications: scoped memory, as suggested by the RTSJ, usage of a real-time GC, or application managed memory through memory pools. However, almost no research has been done into how the Java library which has proven a major part of Java's success, can be used in real-time systems or how it can be adapted to do so. The question of what the best memory management is for the Java standard library remains unanswered.

Java computer: How would a processor architecture and operating system architecture look in a 'Java only' system? Here, we need to rethink our approach to processes, protection, kernel- and user-space, and virtual memory. The standard approach of using memory protection between different processes is necessary for applications that are programmed in languages that use memory addresses as data, i.e. pointer usage and pointer manipulation. In Java, no memory addresses are visible and pointer manipulation is not possible. This very important feature of Java makes Java a *safe* language. Therefore, an error-free JVM means we do not need memory protection between processes and we do not need to make a distinction between kernel and user space (with all the overhead) in a Java system. Another reason for using virtual addresses is link addresses. However, in Java this issue does not exist, as all classes are linked dynamically and the code itself (i.e. the bytecodes) only uses relative addressing.

Another issue here is the paging mechanism in virtual memory system, which has to be redesigned for a Java computer. For this, we need to merge the virtual memory management with the GC. It does not make sense to have a virtual memory manager that works with plain (e.g. 4KB) memory pages without knowledge about object lifetime. We therefore need to incorporate the virtual memory paging with a generational GC. The GC knows which objects have not been accessed for a long time and can be swapped out to the disc. Handling paging as part of the GC process also avoids page fault exceptions and thereby simplifies the processor architecture.

Another question is whether we can substitute the process notation with threads, or whether we need several JVMs on a Java only system. It depends. If we can live with the concept of shared static class members, we can substitute heavyweight processes with lightweight threads. It is also possible that we would have to define some further thread local data structures in the operation system.

It is the opinion of the author that Java is a promising language for future real-time systems. However, a number of issues remain to be solved. JOP, with its time-predictable execution of Java bytecodes, is an important but nevertheless only a small part of a real-time Java system.

Bibliography

[1] Georg Acher. *JIFFY — Ein FPGA-basierter Java Just-in-Time Compiler für eingebettete Anwendungen.* PhD thesis, Technische Universität München, 2003.

[2] aJile Systems Inc. aJ-100 Real-time Low Power Java Processor. preliminary data sheet, 2000.

[3] ARM. Jazelle – ARM Architecture Extensions for Java Applications. white paper.

[4] R. Arnold, F. Mueller, D. Whalley, and M. Harmon. Bounding Worst-Case Instruction Cache Performance. In *IEEE Real-Time Systems Symposium*, pages 172–181, 1994.

[5] Iain Bate, Guillem Bernat, Greg Murphy, and Peter Puschner. Low-Level Analysis of a Portable Java Byte Code WCET Analysis Framework. In *Proc. 7th International Conference on Real-Time Computing Systems and Applications*, pages 39–48, Dec. 2000.

[6] Elliot Berk. JLex: A Lexical Analyzer Generator for Java. Available at http://www.cs.princeton.edu/ appel/modern/java/JLex/.

[7] G. Bernat, A. Burns, and A. Wellings. Portable Worst-Case Execution Time Analysis Using Java Byte Code. In *Proc. 12th EUROMICRO Conference on Real-time Systems*, Jun 2000.

[8] Greg Bollella, James Gosling, Benjamin Brosgol, Peter Dibble, Steve Furr, and Mark Turnbull. *The Real-Time Specification for Java.* Java Series. Addison-Wesley, June 2000.

[9] Ben Brosgol and Brian Dobbing. Real-time Convergence of Ada and Java. In *Proceedings of the 2001 annual ACM SIGAda international conference on Ada*, pages 11–26. ACM Press, 2001.

[10] Alan Burns and Andrew J. Wellings. *Real-Time Systems and Programming Languages: ADA 95, Real-Time Java, and Real-Time POSIX.* Addison-Wesley Longman Publishing Co., Inc., 2001.

[11] J. V. Busquets-Mataix, A. Wellings, J. J. Serrano, R. Ors, and P. Gil. Adding Instruction Cache Effect to Schedulability Analysis of Preemptive Real-Time Systems. In *IEEE Real-Time Technology and Applications Symposium (RTAS '96)*, pages 204–213, Washington - Brussels - Tokyo, June 1996. IEEE Computer Society Press.

[12] Clemens Cap, Dirk Timmermann, Frank Golatowski, Hagen Ploog, Stephan Preuss, and Thomas Geithner. Integration of Java processor core JSM into SmartDev(ices). In *Proceedings of the 8th IEEE International Conference on Emerging Technologies and Factory Automation*, Oktober 2001.

[13] Cyrille Comar, Gary Dismukes, and Franco Gasperoni. Targeting GNAT to the Java Virtual Machine. In *Proceedings of the conference on TRI-Ada '97*, pages 149–161. ACM Press, 1997.

[14] Nazomi Communications. JA 108 Product Brief. Available at http://www.nazomi.com.

[15] Altera Corporation. Nios Soft Core Embedded Processor, ver. 1. data sheet, June 2000.

[16] Altera Corporation. Cyclone FPGA Family Data Sheet, ver. 1.2, April 2003.

[17] Standard Performance Evaluation Corporation. The SPEC JVM98 Benchmark Suite. Available at http://www.spec.org/, August 1998.

[18] Xilinx Corporation. MicroBlaze Processor Reference Guide, EDK v6.2 edition. data sheet, December 2003.

[19] Angelo Corsaro and Douglas C. Schmidt. The Design and Performance of the jRate Real-Time Java Implementation. In *On the Move to Meaningful Internet Systems, 2002 - DOA/CoopIS/ODBASE 2002 Confederated International Conferences DOA, CoopIS and ODBASE 2002*, pages 900–921. Springer-Verlag, 2002.

[20] Angelo Corsaro and Douglas C. Schmidt. Evaluating Real-Time Java Features and Performance for Real-Time Embedded Systems. In *Proceedings of the Eighth IEEE Real-Time and Embedded Technology and Applications Symposium (RTAS'02)*, page 90. IEEE Computer Society, 2002.

[21] Angelo Corsaro and Douglas C. Schmidt. The Design and Performance of Real-Time Java Middleware. *IEEE Transactions on Parallel and Distributed Systems*, 14(11):1155–1167, November 2003.

[22] Martin Delvai, Wolfgang Huber, Peter Puschner, and Andreas Steininger. Processor Support for Temporal Predictability – The SPEAR Design Example. In *Proc. 15th Euromicro International Conference on Real-Time Systems*, Jul. 2003.

[23] S. Dey, P. Sanchez, D. Panigrahi, L. Chen, C. Taylor, and K. Sekar. Using a Soft Core in a SOC Design: Experiences with picoJava. *IEEE Design and Test of Computers*, 17(3):60–71, July 2000.

[24] Brian Dobbing and Alan Burns. The Ravenscar Tasking Profile for High Integrity Real-Time Programs. In *Proceedings of the 1998 annual ACM SIGAda international conference on Ada*, pages 1–6. ACM Press, 1998.

[25] Tom Dowling, James Power, and John Waldron. Relating Static and Dynamic Measurements for the Java Virtual Machine Instruction Set. In N.E. Mastorakis, editor, *Recent Advances in Simulation, Computational Methods and Soft Computing*. WSEAS Press, 2002.

[26] M. Eden and M. Kagan. The Pentium Processor with MMX Technology. In *Proceedings of Compcon '97*, pages 260–262. IEEE Computer Society, 1997.

[27] EJC. The EJC (Embedded Java Controller) platform. Available at http://www.embedded-web.com/index.html.

[28] Jakob Engblom. *Processor Pipelines and Static Worst-Case Execution Time Analysis*. PhD thesis, Uppsala University, 2002.

[29] S. Feizabadi, W. Beebee, B. Ravindran, P. Li, and M. Rinard. Utility Accrual Scheduling with Real-Time Java. *Lecture Notes in Computer Science*, 2889:550–563, 2003.

[30] FLEX. FLEX, a compiler infrastructure written in Java for Java. Available at http://www.flex-compiler.csail.mit.edu/.

[31] Vincent Gay-Para. KJC Kopi Java Compiler. Available at http://www.dms.at/.

[32] C. J. Glossner. *The DEFLT-JAVA Engine*. PhD thesis, Delft University of Technology, 2001.

[33] James Gosling, Bill Joy, Guy Steele, and Gilad Bracha. *The Java Language Specification Second Edition*. The Java Series. Addison-Wesley, Boston, Mass., 2000.

[34] David Gregg, James Power, and John Waldron. Benchmarking the Java Virtual Architecture - The SPECJVM98 Benchmark Suite. In N. Vijaykrishnan and M. Wolczko, editors, *Java Microarchitectures*, pages 1–18. Kluwer Academic, 2002.

[35] Flavius Guian, Per Andersson, Krzysztof Kuchcinski, and Martin Schoeberl. Automatic Generation of Application-Specific Systems Based on a Micro-programmed Java Core. In *Proceedings of the 20th ACM Symposium on Applied Computing, Embedded Systems track*, Santa Fee, New Mexico, March 2005.

[36] Tom R. Halfhill. Imsys Hedges Bets on Java. *Microprocessor Report*, August 2000.

[37] D.S. Hardin. Real-Time Objects on the Bare Metal: An Efficient Hardware Realization of the JavaTM Virtual Machine. In *Proceedings of the Fourth International Symposium on Object-Oriented Real-Time Distributed Computing*, page 53. IEEE Computer Society, 2001.

[38] C.A. Healy, D.B. Whalley, and M.G. Harmon. Integrating the Timing Analysis of Pipelining and Instruction Caching. In *IEEE Real-Time Systems Symposium*, pages 288–297, 1995.

[39] Reinhold Heckmann, Marc Langenbach, Stephan Thesing, and Reinhard Wilhelm. The Influence of Processor Architecture on the Design and Results of WCET Tools. *Proceedings of the IEEE*, 91(7):1038–1054, Jul. 2003.

[40] John Hennessy and David Patterson. *Computer Architecture: A Quantitative Approach, 3rd ed.* Morgan Kaufmann Publishers Inc., Palo Alto, CA 94303, 2002.

[41] Hitachi. Hitachi Single-Chip Microcomputer H8/3297 Series. Hardware Manual.

[42] Imsys AB. ISAJ Reference 2.0, January 2001.

[43] Imsys AB. the Cjip Technical Reference Manual / V0.24, 2003.

[44] Derivation Systems Inc. LavaCORE Configurable Java Processor Core. data sheet, April 2001.

[45] S.A. Ito, L. Carro, and R.P. Jacobi. Making Java Work for Microcontroller Applications. *IEEE Design & Test of Computers*, 18(5):100–110, 2001.

[46] E. Douglas Jensen. A Proposed Initial Approach to Distributed Real-Time Java. In *Third IEEE International Symposium on Object-Oriented Real-Time Distributed Computing (ISORC 2000)*, pages 2–6, March 2000.

[47] Nilsen K., Carnahan L., and Ruark M. Requirements for Real-Time Extensions for the Java Platform. Available at http://www.nist.gov/rt-java/, September 1999.

[48] Kaffe. Kaffe, a complete virtual machine and class library set which allows the execution of Java code. Available at http://www.kaffe.org.

[49] K. B. Kent. *The Co-Disgn of Virtual Machines Using Reconfigurable Hardware*. PhD thesis, University of Victoria, 2003.

[50] A. Kim and J. M. Chang. Designing a Java Microprocessor Core using FPGA Technology. *IEE Computing & Control Engineering Journal*, 11(3):135–141, June 2000.

[51] M. H. Klein, T. Ralya, B. Pollak, and R. Obenza. *A Practitioner's Handbook for Real-Time Analysis : Guide to Rate Monotonic Analysis for Real-Time Systems*. Kluwer Academic Publ., Boston, MA, USA, 1993.

[52] Phillip Koopman. *Stack Computers: The New Wave*. Ellis Horwood, 1989. Out of print, now available over the internet.

[53] Andreas Krall. Efficient JavaVM Just-in-Time Compilation. In *Proceedings of the 1998 International Conference on Parallel Architectures and Compilation Techniques (PACT '98)*, pages 205–212, Paris, October 12–18, 1998. IEEE Computer Society Press.

[54] Andreas Krall and Reinhard Grafl. CACAO – A 64 bit JavaVM Just-in-Time Compiler. In Geoffrey C. Fox and Wei Li, editors, *PPoPP '97 Workshop on Java for Science and Engineering Computation*, Las Vegas, June 1997. ACM.

[55] J. Kreuzinger, U. Brinkschulte, M. Pfeffer, S. Uhrig, and Th. Ungerer. Real-time Event-handling and Scheduling on a Multithreaded Java microcontroller. *Microprocessors and Microsystems*, 27(1):19–31, 2003.

[56] Jagun Kwon, Andy Wellings, and Steve King. Ravenscar-Java: A High Integrity Profile for Real-Time Java. In *Proceedings of the 2002 joint ACM-ISCOPE conference on Java Grande*, pages 131–140. ACM Press, 2002.

[57] Chang-Gun Lee, Joosun Hahn, Yang-Min Seo, Sang Lyul Min, Rhan Ha, Seongsoo Hong, Chang Yun Park, Minsuk Lee, and Chong Sang Kim. Analysis of Cache-Related Preemption Delay in Fixed-Priority Preemptive Scheduling. *IEEE Trans. Comput.*, 47(6):700–713, 1998.

[58] Yau-Tsun Steven Li, Sharad Malik, and Andrew Wolfe. Performance Estimation of Embedded Software with Instruction Cache Modeling. In *Proceedings of the 1995 IEEE/ACM international conference on Computer-aided design*, pages 380–387. IEEE Computer Society, 1995.

[59] Kwei-Jay Lin and Yu-Chung Wang. The Design and Implementation of Teal-Time Schedulers in RED-linux. *Proceedings of the IEEE*, 91(7):1114–1130, July 2003.

[60] Tim Lindholm and Frank Yellin. *The Java Virtual Machine Specification*. Addison-Wesley, Reading, MA, USA, second edition, 1999.

[61] C. L. Liu and James W. Layland. Scheduling Algorithms for Multiprogramming in a Hard-Real-Time Environment. *J. ACM*, 20(1):46–61, 1973.

[62] Digital Communication Technologies Ltd. Lightfoot 32-bit Java Processor Core. data sheet, September 2001.

[63] Vulcan ASIC Ltd. Moon v1.0. data sheet, January 2000.

[64] Vulcan ASIC Ltd. Moon2 - 32 Bit Native Java Technology-Based Processor. product folder, 2003.

[65] Sun Microsystems. A Brief History of the Green Project. Available at: http://today.java.net/jag/old/green/.

[66] Sun Microsystems. Java 2 Platform, Micro Edition (J2ME). Available at: http://java.sun.com/j2me/docs/.

[67] Sun Microsystems. Java Technology: The Early Years. Available at: http://java.sun.com/features/1998/05/birthday.html.

[68] Chuck Moore. ShBoom on ShBoom: A Microcosm of Software and Hardware Tools. In *Proceedings 1990 Rochester Forth Conference*, pages 21–27, New York, June 1990.

[69] M. Mrva, K. Buchenrieder, and R. Kress. A scalable architecture for multi-threaded JAVA applications. In *Proceedings of the conference on Design, automation and test in Europe*, pages 868–874. IEEE Computer Society, 1998.

[70] Albert F. Niessner and Edward G. Benowitz. RTSJ Memory Areas and Their Affects on the Performance of a Flight-Like Attitude Control System. In *Workshop on Java Technologies for Real-Time and Embedded Systems (JTRES), LNCS*, 2003.

[71] K. Nilsen and S. Lee. PERC Real-Time API (Draft 1.3). NewMonics, July 1998.

[72] Anders Nilsson. Compiling Java for Real-Time Systems. Licentiate thesis, Dept. of Computer Science, Lund University, May 2004.

[73] J. Michael O'Connor and Marc Tremblay. picoJava-I: The Java Virtual Machine in Hardware. *IEEE Micro*, 17(2):45–53, 1997.

[74] Krzysztof Palacz, Jason Baker, Chapman Flack, Christian Grothoff, Hiroshi Yamauchi, and Jan Vitek. Engineering a Customizable Intermediate Representation. In *ACM SIGPLAN 2003 Workshop on Interpreters, Virtual Machines and Emulators (IVME 2003)*. ACM SIGPLAN, 2003.

[75] Matthias Pfeffer. *Ein echtzeitfähiges Java-System für einen mehrfädigen Java-Mikrocontroller*. PhD thesis, University of Augsburg, 2000.

[76] James Power and John Waldron. A Method-Level Analysis of Object-Oriented Techniques in Java. Technical Report NUIM-CS-TR-2002-07, Department of Computer Science, NUI Maynooth, Ireland, 2002.

[77] PTSC. IGNITE Processor Brochure, Rev 1.0. Available at http://www.ptsc.com.

[78] P. Puschner and Ch. Koza. Calculating the Maximum Execution Time of Real-Time Programs. *Real-Time Syst.*, 1(2):159–176, 1989.

[79] P. Puschner and A. J. Wellings. A Profile for High Integrity Real-Time Java Programs. In *4th IEEE International Symposium on Object-oriented Real-time distributed Computing (ISORC)*, 2001.

[80] R. Radhakrishnan. *Microarchitectural Techniques to Enable Efficient Java Execution*. PhD thesis, University of Texas at Austin, 2000.

[81] Ramesh Radhakrishnan, N. Vijaykrishnan, Lizy Kurian John, Anand Sivasubramaniam, Juan Rubio, and Jyotsna Sabarinathan. Java Runtime Systems: Characterization and Architectural Implications. *IEEE Trans. Comput.*, 50(2):131–146, 2001.

[82] Mario Aldea Rivas and Michael González Harbour. POSIX-Compatible Application-Defined Scheduling in MaRTE OS. In *Proceedings of the 14th Euromicro Conference on Real-Time Systems*, page 67. IEEE Computer Society, 2002.

[83] Martin Schoeberl. Using a Java Optimized Processor in a Real World Application. In *Proceedings of the First Workshop on Intelligent Solutions in Embedded Systems (WISES 2003)*, pages 165–176, Austria, Vienna, June 2003.

[84] L. Sha, R. Rajkumar, and J. P. Lehoczky. Priority Inheritance Protocols: An Approach to Real-Time Synchronization. *IEEE Trans. Comput.*, 39(9):1175–1185, 1990.

[85] Jose Solorzano. leJOS: Java based OS for Lego RCX. Available at: http://lejos.sourceforge.net/.

[86] International J Consortium Specification. Real-Time Core Extensions, Draft 1.0.14. Available at http://www.j-consortium.org/, September 2000.

[87] International J Consortium Specification. Real-Time Data Access, Release 1.0. Available at http://www.j-consortium.org/, November 2001.

[88] John A. Stankovic. Misconceptions About Real-Time Computing: A Serious Problem for Next-Generation Systems. *Computer*, 21(10):10–19, 1988.

[89] Sun. *picoJava-II Microarchitecture Guide*. Sun Microsystems, March 1999.

[90] Sun. *picoJava-II Programmer's Reference Manual*. Sun Microsystems, March 1999.

[91] Systronix. JStamp Real-Time Native Java Module. data sheet.

[92] TimeSys. Linux RTOS Standard Edition. Available at http://www.timesys.com/.

[93] TimeSys. Real-Time Specification for Java, Reference Implementation. Available at http://www.timesys.com/.

[94] A. Wellings, R. Clark, D. Jensen, and D. Wells. A Framework for Integrating the Real-Time Specification for Java and Java's Remote Method Invocation. In *5th IEEE International Symposium on Object-Oriented Real-Time Distributed Computing (ISORC 2002)*, pages 13–22, April 2002.

[95] R. Zulauf. Entwurf eines Java-Mikrocontrollers und prototypische Implementierung auf einem FPGA. Master's thesis, University of Karlsruhe, 2000.

A Publications

1. Martin Schoeberl. Using a Java Optimized Processor in a Real World Application. In *Proceedings of the First Workshop on Intelligent Solutions in Embedded Systems (WISES 2003)*, pages 165–176, Austria, Vienna, June 2003.

2. Martin Schoeberl. Design Decisions for a Java Processor. In *Tagungsband Austrochip 2003*, pages 115–118, Linz, Austria, October 2003.

3. Martin Schoeberl. JOP: A Java Optimized Processor. In R. Meersman, Z. Tari, and D. Schmidt, editors, *On the Move to Meaningful Internet Systems 2003: Workshop on Java Technologies for Real-Time and Embedded Systems (JTRES 2003)*, volume 2889 of *Lecture Notes in Computer Science*, pages 346–359, Catania, Italy, November 2003. Springer.

4. Martin Schoeberl. Restrictions of Java for Embedded Real-Time Systems. In *Proceedings of the 7th IEEE International Symposium on Object-Oriented Real-Time Distributed Computing (ISORC 2004)*, pages 93–100, Vienna, Austria, May 2004.

5. Martin Schoeberl. Design Rationale of a Processor Architecture for Predictable Real-Time Execution of Java Programs. In *Proceedings of the 10th International Conference on Real-Time and Embedded Computing Systems and Applications (RTCSA 2004)*, Gothenburg, Sweden, August 2004.

6. Martin Schoeberl. Real-Time Scheduling on a Java Processor. In *Proceedings of the 10th International Conference on Real-Time and Embedded Computing Systems and Applications (RTCSA 2004)*, Gothenburg, Sweden, August 2004.

7. Martin Schoeberl. Java Technology in an FPGA. In *Proceedings of the International Conference on Field-Programmable Logic and its applications (FPL 2004)*, Antwerp, Belgium, August 2004.

8. Martin Schoeberl. A Time Predictable Instruction Cache for a Java Processor. In Robert Meersman, Zahir Tari, and Angelo Corsario, editors, *On the Move to Meaningful Internet Systems 2004: Workshop on Java Technologies for Real-Time and Embedded Systems (JTRES 2004)*, volume 3292 of *Lecture*

Notes in Computer Science, pages 371–382, Agia Napa, Cyprus, October 2004. Springer.

9. Flavius Guian, Per Andersson, Krzysztof Kuchcinski, and Martin Schoeberl. Automatic Generation of Application-Specific Systems Based on a Microprogrammed Java Core. To appear in *Proceedings of the 20th ACM Symposium on Applied Computing, Embedded Systems track*, Santa Fee, New Mexico, March 2005.

10. Martin Schoeberl. Design and Implementation of an Efficient Stack Machine. To appear in *Proceedings of the 12th IEEE Reconfigurable Architecture Workshop (RAW2005)*, Denver, Colorado, USA, April 2005. IEEE.

B Acronyms

ADC	Analog to Digital Converter
ALU	Arithmetic and Logic Unit
ASIC	Application-Specific Integrated Circuit
BCET	Best Case Execution Time
CFG	Control Flow Graph
CISC	Complex Instruction Set Computer
CLDC	Connected Limited Device Configuration
CPI	average Clock cycles Per Instruction
CRC	Cyclic Redundancy Check
DMA	Direct Memory Access
DRAM	Dynamic Random Access Memory
EDF	Earliest Deadline First
EMC	Electromagnetic Compatibility
ESD	Electrostatic Discharge
FIFO	Fist In, First Out
FPGA	Field Programmable Gate Array
GC	Garbage Collect(ion/or)
IC	Instruction Count
ILP	Instruction Level Parallelism
JOP	Java Optimized Processor
J2ME	Java2 Micro Edition
J2SE	Java2 Standard Edition
JDK	Java Development Kit
JIT	Just-In-Time
JVM	Java Virtual Machine
LC	Logic Cell
LRU	Least-Recently Used
MBIB	Memory Bytes read per Instruction Byte
MCIB	Memory Cycles per Instruction Byte
MP	Miss Penalty
MTIB	Memory Transactions per Instruction Byte
MUX	Multiplexer

OO	Object Oriented
OS	Operating System
RISC	Reduced Instruction Set Computer
RT	Real-Time
RTOS	Real-Time Operating System
RTSJ	Real-Time Specification for Java
SCADA	Supervisory Control And Data Acquisition
SDRAM	Synchronous DRAM
SRAM	Static Random Access Memory
TOS	Top Of Stack
UART	Universal Asynchronous Receiver/Transmitter
VHDL	Very High Speed Integrated Circuit (VHSIC) Hardware Description Language
WCET	Worst-Case Execution Time

C JOP Instruction Set

The instruction set of JOP, the so-called microcode, is described in this appendix. Each instruction consists of a single instruction word (8 bits) without extra operands and executes in a single cycle[1]. Table C.1 lists the registers and internal memory areas that are used in the dataflow description.

Name	Description
A	Top of the stack
B	The element one below the top of stack
stack[]	The stack buffer for the rest of the stack
sp	The stack pointer for the stack buffer
vp	The variable pointer. Points to the first local in the stack buffer
pc	Microcode program counter
offtbl	Table for branch offsets
jpc	Program counter for the Java bytecode
opd	8 bit operand from the bytecode fetch unit
opd_{16}	16 bit operand from the bytecode fetch unit
ioar	Address register of the IO subsystem
memrda	Read address register of the memory subsystem
memwra	Write address register of the memory subsystem
memrdd	Read data register of the memory subsystem
memwrd	Write data register of the memory subsystem
mula, mulb	Operands of the hardware multiplier
mulr	Result register of the hardware multiplier
membcr	Bytecode address and length register of the memory subsystem
bcstart	Method start address register in the method cache

Table C.1: JOP hardware registers and memory areas

---

[1] The only multicycle instruction is wait and depends on the access time of the external memory

pop

Operation	Pop the top operand stack value
Opcode	00000000
Dataflow	$B \rightarrow A$ $stack[sp] \rightarrow B$ $sp - 1 \rightarrow sp$
JVM equivalent	pop
Description	Pop the top value from the operand stack.

and

Operation	Boolean AND int
Opcode	00000001
Dataflow	$A \wedge B \rightarrow A$ $stack[sp] \rightarrow B$ $sp - 1 \rightarrow sp$
JVM equivalent	iand
Description	Build the bitwise AND (conjunction) of the two top elements of the stack and push back the result onto the operand stack.

or

Operation   Boolean OR int

Opcode   00000010

Dataflow $A \vee B \rightarrow A$
$stack[sp] \rightarrow B$
$sp - 1 \rightarrow sp$

JVM equivalent   ior

Description   Build the bitwise inclusive OR (disjunction) of the two top elements of the stack and push back the result onto the operand stack.

xor

Operation   Boolean XOR int

Opcode   00000011

Dataflow $A \not\equiv B \rightarrow A$
$stack[sp] \rightarrow B$
$sp - 1 \rightarrow sp$

JVM equivalent   ixor

Description   Build the bitwise exclusive OR (negation of equivalence) of the two top elements of the stack and push back the result onto the operand stack.

add

Operation   Add int

Opcode   00000100

Dataflow $A + B \rightarrow A$
                     $stack[sp] \rightarrow B$
                     $sp - 1 \rightarrow sp$

JVM equivalent   iadd

Description   Add the two top elements from the stack and push back the result onto the operand stack.

sub

Operation   Subtract int

Opcode   00000101

Dataflow $A - B \rightarrow A$
                     $stack[sp] \rightarrow B$
                     $sp - 1 \rightarrow sp$

JVM equivalent   isub

Description   Subtract the two top elements from the stack and push back the result onto the operand stack.

stioa

Operation	Store IO address
Opcode	00001000
Dataflow	$A \rightarrow ioar$
	$B \rightarrow A$
	$stack[sp] \rightarrow B$
	$sp - 1 \rightarrow sp$

JVM equivalent

Description   The top value from the stack is stored in the IO address register. This address is used on following read (ldiod) and write (stiod) operations.

stiod

Operation	Store IO data
Opcode	00001001
Dataflow	$A \rightarrow io\ device$
	$B \rightarrow A$
	$stack[sp] \rightarrow B$
	$sp - 1 \rightarrow sp$

JVM equivalent

Description   The top value from the stack is stored in the IO device. The IO device is selected by the previous stioa.

stmra

Operation   Store memory read address

Opcode   00001010

Dataflow $A \rightarrow memrda$
                       $B \rightarrow A$
                       $stack[sp] \rightarrow B$
                       $sp - 1 \rightarrow sp$

JVM equivalent

Description   The top value from the stack is stored as read address in the
                       memory subsystem. This operation starts the concurrent mem-
                       ory read. The processor can continue with other operations.
                       When the datum is needed a `wait` instruction stalls the pro-
                       cessor till the read access is finished. The value is read with
                       `ldmrd`.

stmwa

Operation   Store memory write address

Opcode   00001011

Dataflow $A \rightarrow memwra$
                       $B \rightarrow A$
                       $stack[sp] \rightarrow B$
                       $sp - 1 \rightarrow sp$

JVM equivalent

Description   The top value from the stack is stored as write address in the
                       memory subsystem for a following `stmwd`.

stmwd

Operation	Store memory write data
Opcode	`00001100`
Dataflow	$A \to memwrd$
	$B \to A$
	$stack[sp] \to B$
	$sp - 1 \to sp$

JVM equivalent

Description The top value from the stack is stored as write data in the memory subsystem. This operation starts the concurrent memory write The processor can continue with other operations. The wait instruction stalls the processor till the write access is finished.

stmul

Operation	Multiply int
Opcode	`00001101`
Dataflow	$A \to mula$
	$B \to mulb$
	$B \to A$
	$stack[sp] \to B$
	$sp - 1 \to sp$

JVM equivalent

Description The top value from the stack is stored as first operand for the multiplier. The value one below the top of stack is stored as second operand for the multiplier. This operation starts the multiplier. The result is read with the ldmul instruction.

stbcrd

Operation	Start bytecode read
Opcode	00001111
Dataflow	$A \rightarrow membcr$ $B \rightarrow A$ $stack[sp] \rightarrow B$ $sp - 1 \rightarrow sp$
JVM equivalent	
Description	The top value from the stack is stored as address and length of a method in the memory subsystem. This operation starts the memory transfer from the main memory to the bytecode cache (DMA). The processor can continue with other operations. The wait instruction stalls the processor till the transfer has finished. No other memory accesses are allowed during the bytecode read.

st<n>

Operation	Store 32-bit word into local variable
Opcode	000100nn
Dataflow	$A \rightarrow stack[vp + n]$ $B \rightarrow A$ $stack[sp] \rightarrow B$ $sp - 1 \rightarrow sp$
JVM equivalent	astore_<n>, istore_<n>, fstore_<n>
Description	The value on the top of the operand stack is popped and stored in the local variable at position *n*.

st

Operation   Store 32-bit word into local variable

Opcode   00010101

Dataflow $A \rightarrow stack[vp + opd]$
                     $B \rightarrow A$
                     $stack[sp] \rightarrow B$
                     $sp - 1 \rightarrow sp$

JVM equivalent   astore, istore, fstore

Description   The value on the top of the operand stack is popped and stored in the local variable at position *opd*. *opd* is taken from the bytecode instruction stream.

stvp

Operation   Store variable pointer

Opcode   00011000

Dataflow $A \rightarrow vp$
                     $B \rightarrow A$
                     $stack[sp] \rightarrow B$
                     $sp - 1 \rightarrow sp$

JVM equivalent

Description   The value on the top of the operand stack is popped and stored in the variable pointer (vp).

stjpc

Operation	Store Java program counter
Opcode	00011001
Dataflow	$A \rightarrow jpc$ $B \rightarrow A$ $stack[sp] \rightarrow B$ $sp - 1 \rightarrow sp$

JVM equivalent

Description The value on the top of the operand stack is popped and stored in the Java program counter (jpc).

stsp

Operation	Store stack pointer
Opcode	00011011
Dataflow	$A \rightarrow sp$ $B \rightarrow A$ $stack[sp] \rightarrow B$

JVM equivalent

Description The value on the top of the operand stack is popped and stored in the stack pointer (sp).

ushr

Operation	Logical shift rigth `int`
Opcode	00011100
Dataflow	$B >>> A \rightarrow A$ $stack[sp] \rightarrow B$ $sp - 1 \rightarrow sp$
JVM equivalent	`iushr`
Description	The values are popped from the operand stack. An `int` result is calculated by shifting the TOS-1 value rigth by s position, with zero extension, where s is the value of the low 5 bits of the TOS. The result is pushed onto the operand stack.

shl

Operation	Shift left `int`
Opcode	00011101
Dataflow	$B << A \rightarrow A$ $stack[sp] \rightarrow B$ $sp - 1 \rightarrow sp$
JVM equivalent	`ishl`
Description	The values are popped from the operand stack. An `int` result is calculated by shifting the TOS-1 value left by s position, where s is the value of the low 5 bits of the TOS. The result is pushed onto the operand stack.

shr

Operation	Arithmetic shift rigth `int`
Opcode	`00011110`
Dataflow	$B >> A \rightarrow A$
	$stack[sp] \rightarrow B$
	$sp - 1 \rightarrow sp$
JVM equivalent	`ishr`
Description	The values are popped from the operand stack. An `int` result is calculated by shifting the TOS-1 value rigth by s position, with sign extension, where s is the value of the low 5 bits of the TOS. The result is pushed onto the operand stack.

stm

Operation	Store in local memory
Opcode	`001nnnnn`
Dataflow	$A \rightarrow stack[n]$
	$B \rightarrow A$
	$stack[sp] \rightarrow B$
	$sp - 1 \rightarrow sp$
JVM equivalent	
Description	The top value from the operand stack is stored in the local memory (stack) at position n. These 32 memory destinations represent microcode local variables.

bz

Operation	Branch if value is zero
Opcode	010nnnnn
Dataflow	if $A = 0$ then $pc + offtbl[n] + 2 \to pc$ $B \to A$ $stack[sp] \to B$ $sp - 1 \to sp$
JVM equivalent	
Description	If the top value from the operand stack is zero a microcode branch is taken. The value is popped from the operand stack. Due to a pipeline delay, the zero flag is delayed one cycle, i.e. the value from the last but one instruction is taken. The branch is followed by two branch delay slots. The branch offset is taken from the table $offtbl$ indexed by n.

bnz

Operation	Branch if value is not zero
Opcode	011nnnnn
Dataflow	if $A \neq 0$ then $pc + offtbl[n] + 2 \rightarrow pc$ $B \rightarrow A$ $stack[sp] \rightarrow B$ $sp - 1 \rightarrow sp$
JVM equivalent	
Description	If the top value from the operand stack is not zero a microcode branch is taken. The value is popped from the operand stack. Due to a pipeline delay, the zero flag is delayed one cycle, i.e. the value from the last but one instruction is taken. The branch is followed by two branch delay slots. The branch offset is taken from the table *offtbl* indexed by *n*.

nop

Operation	Do nothing
Opcode	10000000
Dataflow	—
JVM equivalent	nop
Description	The famous no operation instruction.

wait

Operation	Wait for memory completion
Opcode	10000001
Dataflow	—
JVM equivalent	
Description	This instruction stalls the processor until a pending memory instruction (stmra, stmwd or stbcrd) has completed. Two consecutive wait instructions are necessary for a correct stall of the decode and execute stage.

jbr

Operation	Conditional bytecode branch and goto
Opcode	10000010
Dataflow	—
JVM equivalent	ifnull, ifnonnull, ifeq, ifne, iflt, ifge, ifgt, ifle, if_acmpeq, if_acmpne, if_icmpeq, if_icmpne, if_icmplt, if_icmpge, if_icmpgt, if_icmple, goto
Description	Execute a bytecode branch or goto. The branch condition and offset are calculated in the bytecode fetch unit. Arguments must be removed with pop instructions in the following microcode instructions.

ldm

Operation	Load from local memory
Opcode	101nnnnn
Dataflow	$stack[n] \rightarrow A$ $A \rightarrow B$ $B \rightarrow stack[sp+1]$ $sp+1 \rightarrow sp$
JVM equivalent	
Description	The value from the local memory (stack) at position n is pushed onto the operand stack. These 32 memory destinations represent microcode local variables.

ldi

Operation	Load from local memory
Opcode	110nnnnn
Dataflow	$stack[n+32] \rightarrow A$ $A \rightarrow B$ $B \rightarrow stack[sp+1]$ $sp+1 \rightarrow sp$
JVM equivalent	
Description	The value from the local memory (stack) at position $n+32$ is pushed onto the operand stack. These 32 memory destinations represent microcode constants.

ldiod

Operation	Load IO data
Opcode	11100001
Dataflow	$io\ device \rightarrow A$ $A \rightarrow B$ $B \rightarrow stack[sp+1]$ $sp+1 \rightarrow sp$
JVM equivalent	
Description	The value from the IO device is pushed onto the operand stack. The IO device is selected by the previous stioa.

ldmrd

Operation	Load memory read data
Opcode	11100010
Dataflow	$memrdd \rightarrow A$ $A \rightarrow B$ $B \rightarrow stack[sp+1]$ $sp+1 \rightarrow sp$

JVM equivalent

Description   The value from the memory system after a memory read is pushed onto the operand stack. This operation is usually preceded by two `wait` instructions.

ldmul

Operation	Load multiplier result
Opcode	11100101
Dataflow	$mulr \rightarrow A$ $A \rightarrow B$ $B \rightarrow stack[sp+1]$ $sp+1 \rightarrow sp$

JVM equivalent   (`imul`)

Description   The result of the multiplier is pushed onto the operand stack.

ldbcstart

Operation	Load method start
Opcode	11100111

Dataflow

$bcstart \rightarrow A$
$A \rightarrow B$
$B \rightarrow stack[sp + 1]$
$sp + 1 \rightarrow sp$

JVM equivalent

Description   The method start address in the method cache is pushed onto the operand stack.

ld<n>

Operation	Load 32-bit word from local variable
Opcode	111010nn

Dataflow

$stack[vp + n] \rightarrow A$
$A \rightarrow B$
$B \rightarrow stack[sp + 1]$
$sp + 1 \rightarrow sp$

JVM equivalent   aload_<n>, iload_<n>, fload_<n>

Description   The local variable at position n is pushed onto the operand stack.

ld

Operation   Load 32-bit word from local variable

Opcode   11101101

Dataflow $stack[vp + opd] \rightarrow A$
                         $A \rightarrow B$
                         $B \rightarrow stack[sp + 1]$
                         $sp + 1 \rightarrow sp$

JVM equivalent   aload, iload, fload

Description   The local variable at position opd is pushed onto the operand
                         stack. opd is taken from the bytecode instruction stream.

ldsp

Operation   Load stack pointer

Opcode   11110000

Dataflow $sp \rightarrow A$
                         $A \rightarrow B$
                         $B \rightarrow stack[sp + 1]$
                         $sp + 1 \rightarrow sp$

JVM equivalent

Description   The stack pointer is pushed onto the operand stack.

ldvp

Operation	Load variable pointer
Opcode	11110001
Dataflow	$vp \rightarrow A$ $A \rightarrow B$ $B \rightarrow stack[sp+1]$ $sp+1 \rightarrow sp$

JVM equivalent

Description	The variable pointer is pushed onto the operand stack.

ldjpc

Operation	Load Java program counter
Opcode	11110010
Dataflow	$jpc \rightarrow A$ $A \rightarrow B$ $B \rightarrow stack[sp+1]$ $sp+1 \rightarrow sp$

JVM equivalent

Description	The Java program counter is pushed onto the operand stack.

ld_opd_8u

Operation   Load 8-bit bytecode operand unsigned

Opcode   11110100

Dataflow $opd \rightarrow A$
                     $A \rightarrow B$
                     $B \rightarrow stack[sp+1]$
                     $sp+1 \rightarrow sp$

JVM equivalent

Description   A single byte from the bytecode stream is pushed as int onto
                     the operand stack.

ld_opd_8s

Operation   Load 8-bit bytecode operand signed

Opcode   11110101

Dataflow $opd \rightarrow A$
                     $A \rightarrow B$
                     $B \rightarrow stack[sp+1]$
                     $sp+1 \rightarrow sp$

JVM equivalent   (bipush)

Description   A single byte from the bytecode stream is sign-extended to an
                     int and pushed onto the operand stack.

ld_opd_16u

Operation	Load 16-bit bytecode operand unsigned
Opcode	11110110

Dataflow

$opd\_16 \rightarrow A$
$A \rightarrow B$
$B \rightarrow stack[sp + 1]$
$sp + 1 \rightarrow sp$

JVM equivalent

Description   A 16-bit word from the bytecode stream is pushed as int onto the operand stack.

ld_opd_16s

Operation	Load 16-bit bytecode operand signed
Opcode	11110111

Dataflow

$opd\_16 \rightarrow A$
$A \rightarrow B$
$B \rightarrow stack[sp + 1]$
$sp + 1 \rightarrow sp$

JVM equivalent   (sipush)

Description   A 16-bit word from the bytecode stream is sign-extended to an int and pushed onto the operand stack.

dup

Operation   Duplicate the top operand stack value

Opcode   `11111000`

Dataflow $A \rightarrow B$
                     $B \rightarrow stack[sp+1]$
                     $sp + 1 \rightarrow sp$

JVM equivalent   dup

Description   Duplicate the top value on the operand stack and push it onto
                     the operand stack.

D Bytecode Execution Time

Table D.1 lists the bytecodes of the JVM with their opcode, mnemonics, the implementation type and the execution time on JOP. In the implementation column *hw* means that this bytecode has a microcode equivalent, *mc* means that a microcode sequence implements the bytecode, *Java* means the bytecode is implemented in Java, and a '-' indicates that this bytecode is not yet implemented. For bytecodes with a variable execution time the minimum and maximum values are given.

Opcode	Instruction	Implementation	Cycles
0	nop	hw	1
1	aconst_null	hw	1
2	iconst_m1	hw	1
3	iconst_0	hw	1
4	iconst_1	hw	1
5	iconst_2	hw	1
6	iconst_3	hw	1
7	iconst_4	hw	1
8	iconst_5	hw	1
9	lconst_0	mc	2
10	lconst_1	mc	2
11	fconst_0	-	
12	fconst_1	-	
13	fconst_2	-	
14	dconst_0	-	
15	dconst_1	-	
16	bipush	mc	2
17	sipush	mc	3
18	ldc	mc	3+r
19	ldc_w	mc	4+r
20	ldc2_w[20]	mc	8+2*r
21	iload	mc	2
22	lload	mc	11

Table D.1: Implemented bytecodes and execution time in cycles

Opcode	Instruction	Implementation	Cycles
23	fload	mc	2
24	dload	mc	11
25	aload	mc	2
26	iload_0	hw	1
27	iload_1	hw	1
28	iload_2	hw	1
29	iload_3	hw	1
30	lload_0	mc	2
31	lload_1	mc	2
32	lload_2	mc	2
33	lload_3	mc	11
34	fload_0	hw	1
35	fload_1	hw	1
36	fload_2	hw	1
37	fload_3	hw	1
38	dload_0	mc	2
39	dload_1	mc	2
40	dload_2	mc	2
41	dload_3	mc	11
42	aload_0	hw	1
43	aload_1	hw	1
44	aload_2	hw	1
45	aload_3	hw	1
46	iaload[46]	mc	19+2*r
47	laload	-	
48	faload[46]	mc	19+2*r
49	daload	-	
50	aaload[46]	mc	19+2*r
51	baload[46]	mc	19+2*r
52	caload[46]	mc	19+2*r
53	saload[46]	mc	19+2*r
54	istore	mc	2
55	lstore	mc	11
56	fstore	mc	2
57	dstore	mc	11
58	astore	mc	2

Table D.1: Implemented bytecodes and execution time in cycles

Opcode	Instruction	Implementation	Cycles
59	istore_0	hw	1
60	istore_1	hw	1
61	istore_2	hw	1
62	istore_3	hw	1
63	lstore_0	mc	2
64	lstore_1	mc	2
65	lstore_2	mc	2
66	lstore_3	mc	11
67	fstore_0	hw	1
68	fstore_1	hw	1
69	fstore_2	hw	1
70	fstore_3	hw	1
71	dstore_0	mc	2
72	dstore_1	mc	2
73	dstore_2	mc	2
74	dstore_3	mc	11
75	astore_0	hw	1
76	astore_1	hw	1
77	astore_2	hw	1
78	astore_3	hw	1
79	iastore[79]	mc	22+r+w
80	lastore	-	
81	fastore[79]	mc	22+r+w
82	dastore	-	
83	aastore[79]	mc	22+r+w
84	bastore[79]	mc	22+r+w
85	castore[79]	mc	22+r+w
86	sastore[79]	mc	22+r+w
87	pop	hw	1
88	pop2	mc	2
89	dup	hw	1
90	dup_x1	mc	5
91	dup_x2	-	
92	dup2	mc	6
93	dup2_x1	-	
94	dup2_x2	-	

Table D.1: Implemented bytecodes and execution time in cycles

Opcode	Instruction	Implementation	Cycles
95	swap	-	
96	iadd	hw	1
97	ladd	Java	
98	fadd	Java	
99	dadd	-	
100	isub	hw	1
101	lsub	Java	
102	fsub	Java	
103	dsub	-	
104	imul	mc	35
105	lmul	-	
106	fmul	-	
107	dmul	-	
108	idiv	Java	
109	ldiv	-	
110	fdiv	-	
111	ddiv	-	
112	irem	Java	
113	lrem	-	
114	frem	-	
115	drem	-	
116	ineg	mc	4
117	lneg	Java	
118	fneg	-	
119	dneg	-	
120	ishl	hw	1
121	lshl	-	
122	ishr	hw	1
123	lshr	-	
124	iushr	hw	1
125	lushr	Java	
126	iand	hw	1
127	land	-	
128	ior	hw	1
129	lor	-	
130	ixor	hw	1

Table D.1: Implemented bytecodes and execution time in cycles

Opcode	Instruction	Implementation	Cycles
131	lxor	Java	
132	iinc	mc	11
133	i2l	Java	
134	i2f	-	
135	i2d	-	
136	l2i	mc	3
137	l2f	-	
138	l2d	-	
139	f2i	-	
140	f2l	-	
141	f2d	-	
142	d2i	-	
143	d2l	-	
144	d2f	-	
145	i2b	-	
146	i2c	mc	2
147	i2s	-	
148	lcmp	Java	
149	fcmpl	-	
150	fcmpg	-	
151	dcmpl	-	
152	dcmpg	-	
153	ifeq	mc	4
154	ifne	mc	4
155	iflt	mc	4
156	ifge	mc	4
157	ifgt	mc	4
158	ifle	mc	4
159	if_icmpeq	mc	4
160	if_icmpne	mc	4
161	if_icmplt	mc	4
162	if_icmpge	mc	4
163	if_icmpgt	mc	4
164	if_icmple	mc	4
165	if_acmpeq	mc	4
166	if_acmpne	mc	4

Table D.1: Implemented bytecodes and execution time in cycles

Opcode	Instruction	Implementation	Cycles
167	goto	mc	4
168	jsr	-	
169	ret	-	
170	tableswitch[170]	Java	
171	lookupswitch[171]	Java	
172	ireturn[172]	mc	15+r+b
173	lreturn[173]	mc	17+r+b
174	freturn[172]	mc	15+r+b
175	dreturn[173]	mc	17+r+b
176	areturn[172]	mc	15+r+b
177	return[177]	mc	13+r+b
178	getstatic	mc	4+2*r
179	putstatic	mc	5+r+w
180	getfield	mc	10+2*r
181	putfield	mc	13+r+w
182	invokevirtual[182]	mc	78+4*r+b
183	invokespecial[183]	mc	58+3*r+b
184	invokestatic[183]	mc	58+3*r+b
185	invokeinterface[185]	mc	84+6*r+b
186	unused_ba	-	
187	new[187]	Java	
188	newarray[188]	mc	12+w
189	anewarray	Java	
190	arraylength	mc	2+r
191	athrow	-	
192	checkcast	-	
193	instanceof	-	
194	monitorenter	hw	9
195	monitorexit	hw	10/11
196	wide	-	
197	multianewarray	-	
198	ifnull	hw	4
199	ifnonnull	hw	4
200	goto_w	-	
201	jsr_w	-	
202	breakpoint	-	

Table D.1: Implemented bytecodes and execution time in cycles

Opcode	Instruction	Implementation	Cycles
203	reserved	-	
204	reserved	-	
205	reserved	-	
206	reserved	-	
207	reserved	-	
208	reserved	-	
209	jopsys_rd	mc	3
210	jopsys_wr	mc	3
211	jopsys_rdmem	mc	r
212	jopsys_wrmem	mc	w+1
213	jopsys_rdint	mc	8
214	jopsys_wrint	mc	8
215	jopsys_getsp	mc	3
216	jopsys_setsp	mc	4
217	jopsys_getvp	hw	1
218	jopsys_setvp	mc	2
219	jopsys_int2ext[219]	mc	$12+n*(19+w)$
220	jopsys_ext2int[220]	mc	$12+n*(19+w)$
221	jopsys_nop	mc	1
222	reserved	-	
223	reserved	-	
224	reserved	-	
225	reserved	-	
226	reserved	-	
227	reserved	-	
228	reserved	-	
229	reserved	-	
230	reserved	-	
231	reserved	-	
232	reserved	-	
233	reserved	-	
234	reserved	-	
235	reserved	-	
236	reserved	-	
237	reserved	-	
238	reserved	-	

Table D.1: Implemented bytecodes and execution time in cycles

Opcode	Instruction	Implementation	Cycles
239	reserved	-	
240	sys_int	Java	
241	reserved	-	
242	reserved	-	
243	reserved	-	
244	reserved	-	
245	reserved	-	
246	reserved	-	
247	reserved	-	
248	reserved	-	
249	reserved	-	
250	reserved	-	
251	reserved	-	
252	reserved	-	
253	reserved	-	
254	reserved	-	
255	reserved	-	

Table D.1: Implemented bytecodes and execution time in cycles

The bytecodes that access memory are indicated by an r for a memory read and an w for a memory write at the cycles column. The cycles for the memory access have to be added to the execution time. These two values are implementation dependent (clock frequency versus RAM access time, data bus width); for the Cyclone EP1C6 board with 15ns SRAMs and 100MHz clock frequency these values are both 6 cycles (3 cycles for the memory access and 3 cycles due to pipeline delays). The memory access time for the bytecode load a is 3 clock cycles for this board.

For some bytecodes, part of the memory latency can be hidden by executing microcode during the memory access. However, these cycles can only be subtracted when the memory access time (r or w) is longer than 4 cycles. The exact execution time with the subtraction of the saved cycles is given in the footnote.

On a method invoke or return the bytecode has to be loaded into the cache on a

---

[20] The exact value is $8 + r + \begin{cases} r-2 & : & r \geq 6 \\ 4 & : & r < 6 \end{cases}$

[46] The exact value is $19 + r + \begin{cases} r-2 & : & r \geq 6 \\ 4 & : & r < 6 \end{cases}$

[79] The exact value is $22 + \begin{cases} r-2 & : & r \geq 6 \\ 4 & : & r < 6 \end{cases} + w$

[170] tableswitch execution time depends to a great extent on the caching of the corresponding Java method or the memory transfer time for the method.

[171] lookupswitch execution time depends to a great extent on the caching of the corresponding Java method or the memory transfer time for the method. lookupswitch also depends on the argument as it performs a linear search in the jump table.

[172] The exact value is: $15 + \begin{cases} r-3 & : & r \geq 7 \\ 4 & : & r < 7 \end{cases} + \begin{cases} b-8 & : & b \geq 8 \\ 0 & : & b < 8 \end{cases}$

[173] The exact value is: $15 + \begin{cases} r-3 & : & r \geq 7 \\ 4 & : & r < 7 \end{cases} + \begin{cases} b-9 & : & b \geq 9 \\ 0 & : & b < 9 \end{cases}$

[177] The exact value is: $13 + \begin{cases} r-3 & : & r \geq 7 \\ 4 & : & r < 7 \end{cases} + \begin{cases} b-7 & : & b \geq 7 \\ 0 & : & b < 7 \end{cases}$

[182] The exact value is: $78 + 2r + \begin{cases} r-3 & : & r \geq 7 \\ 4 & : & r < 7 \end{cases} + \begin{cases} r-2 & : & r \geq 6 \\ 4 & : & r < 6 \end{cases} + \begin{cases} b-39 & : & b \geq 39 \\ 0 & : & b < 39 \end{cases}$

[183] The exact value is: $58 + r + \begin{cases} r-3 & : & r \geq 7 \\ 4 & : & r < 7 \end{cases} + \begin{cases} r-2 & : & r \geq 6 \\ 4 & : & r < 6 \end{cases} + \begin{cases} b-39 & : & b \geq 39 \\ 0 & : & b < 39 \end{cases}$

[185] The exact value is: $84 + 4r + \begin{cases} r-3 & : & r \geq 7 \\ 4 & : & r < 7 \end{cases} + \begin{cases} r-2 & : & r \geq 6 \\ 4 & : & r < 6 \end{cases} + \begin{cases} b-39 & : & b \geq 39 \\ 0 & : & b < 39 \end{cases}$

[187] new execution time depends to a great extent on the caching of the corresponding Java method or the memory transfer time for the method. new also depends on the size of the created object as the memory for the object is filled with zeros.

[188] The time to clear the array is not included.

[219] The exact value is $12 + n(19 + \begin{cases} w-8 & : & w \geq 12 \\ 4 & : & w < 12 \end{cases})$. n is the number of words transferred.

[220] The exact value is $12 + n(19 + \begin{cases} w-10 & : & w \geq 14 \\ 4 & : & w < 14 \end{cases})$. n is the number of words transferred.

cache miss. The load time b is:

$$b = \begin{cases} 2+(n+1)a & : \quad \text{cache miss} \\ 0 & : \quad \text{cach hit} \end{cases}$$

with n as the length of the method in number of 32-bit words. For short methods the load time of the method on a cache miss, or part of it, is hidden by microcode execution. The exact value is given in the footnote.

E Benchmark Results

	JOP	leJOS	TINI	Komodo	JStamp
Frequency [MHz]	100	16	40	33	73.728
iload iadd	49,344,000	19,140	50,724	4,111,569	1,934,642
iinc	9,078,000	37,925	103,044	8,318,030	1,789,378
ldc	10,010,000	11,941	35,463	825,446	1,101,445
if_icmplt taken	16,644,000	9,941	31,629	1,372,264	1,747,626
if_icmplt not taken	16,710,000	10,529	33,032	1,375,754	1,833,174
getfield	4,002,000	8,515	16,684	687,877	518,071
getstatic	5,874,000	9,547	8,962	412,723	723,155
iaload	3,328,000	14,787	25,924	1,180,501	992,969
invoke	781,935	3,362	6,159	85,874	211,406
invoke static	989,222	4,129	6,815	48,510	271,933
invoke interface	684,896	3,141	5,885	20402	138,847
Sieve	4,286	7	15	627	564
Kfl	14,222	25	64	924	2,221
UDP/IP	6,050	13	29	520	1,004
geom. Mean App	9,276	18	43	693	1,493
geom. Mean App/MHz	79	1	1	21	20

Table E.1: Raw data of all benchmarks in [iterations/s] I.

	SaJe	EJC	Sun jvm	gcj	Xint
Frequency [MHz]	103	74	266	266	266
iload iadd	12,710,000	72,315,000	84,307,000	248,551,000	15,363,000
iinc	9,320,000	36,002,000	296,941,000	88,069,000	122,228,000
ldc	11,275,000	23,967,000	132,626,000		8,719,000
if_icmplt taken	5,652,000	35,925,000	128,561,000	86,480,000	7,449,000
if_icmplt not taken	7,281,000	71,697,000	246,723,000	89,240,000	7,206,000
getfield	4,433,000	7,212,000	90,687,000	122,016,000	6,853,000
getstatic	6,786,000	17,962,000	86,703,000	241,398,000	6,700,000
iaload	7,854,000	5,966,000	65,536,000	23,967,000	8,962,000
invoke	894,689	1,703,000	10,022,000	20,092,000	1,458,381
invoke static	1,084,359	309,132	270,600,000	7,898,000	1,620,673
invoke interface	674,759	1,598,000	10,010,000	5,588,000	1,381,523
Sieve	3,972	9,475	52,681	39,432	6,601
Kfl	14,148	9,893	212,952	139,884	17,310
UDP/IP	6,415	2,822	91,851	38,460	8,747
geom. Mean App	9,527	5,284	139,857	73,348	12,305
App/MHz	92	71	526	276	46

Table E.2: Raw data of all benchmarks in [iterations/s] II.

| Type | Size | MBIB | MTIB | Memory access time | | |
				SRAM	SDRAM	DDR
Prefetch buffer	8 B	1.37	0.342	1.02	2.05	1.71
Single method cache	1 KB	2.32	0.021	1.18	0.69	0.39
Two block cache	2 KB	1.21	0.013	0.62	0.37	0.21
Four block cache	4 KB	0.90	0.010	0.46	0.27	0.16
Direct-mapped 8 bytes	1 KB	0.28	0.035	0.18	0.25	0.19
Direct-mapped 16 bytes	1 KB	0.38	0.024	0.22	0.22	0.16
Direct-mapped 32 bytes	1 KB	0.58	0.018	0.31	0.24	0.15
Direct-mapped 8 bytes	2 KB	0.17	0.022	0.11	0.15	0.12
Direct-mapped 16 bytes	2 KB	0.25	0.015	0.14	0.14	0.10
Direct-mapped 32 bytes	2 KB	0.41	0.013	0.22	0.17	0.11
Direct-mapped 8 bytes	4 KB	0.00	0.001	0.00	0.00	0.00
Direct-mapped 16 bytes	4 KB	0.01	0.000	0.00	0.00	0.00
Direct-mapped 32 bytes	4 KB	0.01	0.000	0.00	0.00	0.00
Variable block cache 8 blocks	1 KB	0.80	0.009	0.41	0.24	0.14
Variable block cache 16 blocks	1 KB	0.71	0.008	0.36	0.22	0.12
Variable block cache 32 blocks	1 KB	0.70	0.008	0.36	0.21	0.12
Variable block cache 64 blocks	1 KB	0.70	0.008	0.36	0.21	0.12
Variable block cache 8 blocks	2 KB	0.73	0.008	0.37	0.22	0.13
Variable block cache 16 blocks	2 KB	0.37	0.004	0.19	0.11	0.06
Variable block cache 32 blocks	2 KB	0.24	0.003	0.12	0.08	0.04
Variable block cache 64 blocks	2 KB	0.12	0.001	0.06	0.04	0.02
Variable block cache 8 blocks	4 KB	0.73	0.008	0.37	0.22	0.13
Variable block cache 16 blocks	4 KB	0.25	0.003	0.13	0.08	0.05
Variable block cache 32 blocks	4 KB	0.01	0.000	0.00	0.00	0.00
Variable block cache 64 blocks	4 KB	0.00	0.000	0.00	0.00	0.00

Table E.3: Cache performance in MBIB and MTIB of all variations of the method cache and a conventional direct-mapped cache. Average memory access time per instruction byte for three different main memory technologies. Memory access times are in clock cycles.

F Cyclone FPGA Board

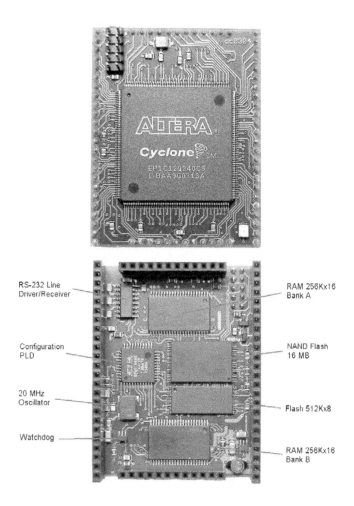

Figure F.1: Top and bottom side of the Cyclone FPGA board

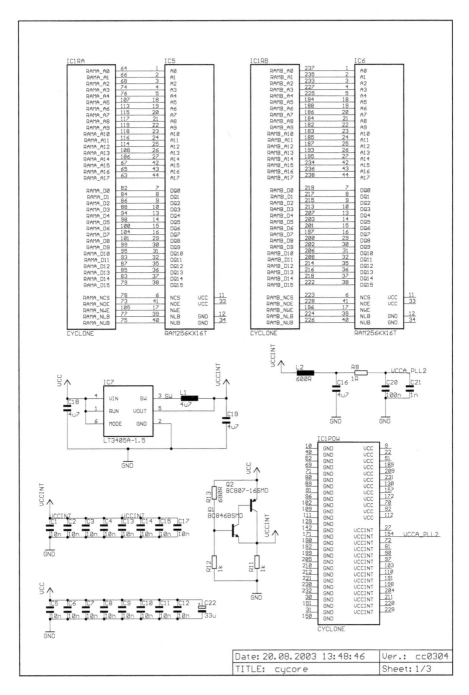

Figure F.2: Schematic of the Cyclone FPGA board, page 1

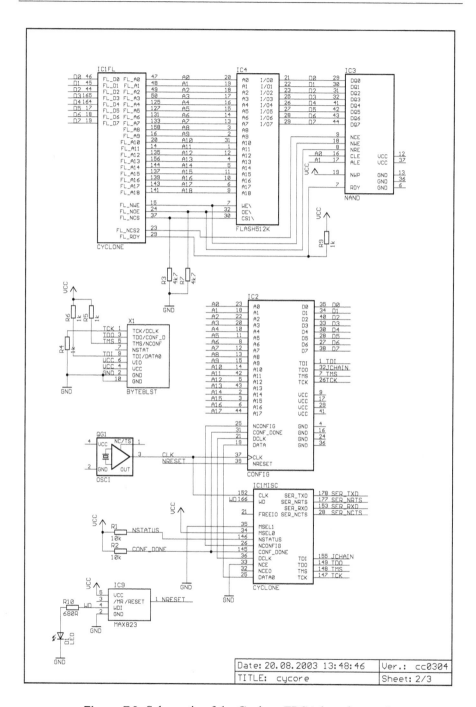

Figure F.3: Schematic of the Cyclone FPGA board, page 2

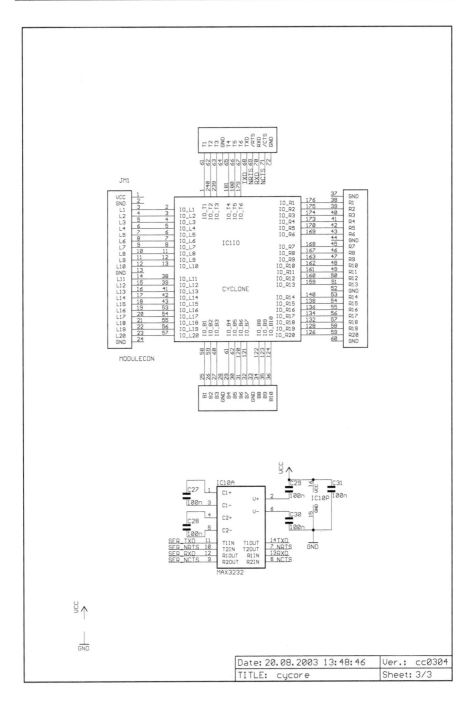

Figure F.4: Schematic of the Cyclone FPGA board, page 3